The Net Bible

Richard Longhurst
Nick Merritt

.net

Future Publishing Limited
Beauford Court, 30 Monmouth Street, Bath BA1 2BW

ISBN 1-85981-165-5

Editing, Design & Layout The Book Factory
Cover Design Jez Bridgeman

Printed and bound in the UK by Redwood Press

The Net Bible

Chapter 1
Introduction

Chapter 1
Introduction   9

Why do you want to get on-line?   10
Why are you telling me this?   12
Where has it come from?   13
Who's in charge?   15
What does that mean to me?   17
Blimey, whatever next?   17
The History of the Internet   19

Chapter 2
Choosing a modem

Chapter 2
Choosing a modem   21

What's all this about?   22
That was a bit heavy...   24
So which one should I buy?   26
We recommend...   28

Chapter 3
Choosing a Net Service Provider

Chapter 3
**Choosing a Net
Service Provider**   31

Work out where you are   32
What do you want to do with it?   33
What about software?   34

And the modem at the other end?   35
How will you be paying?   36
A reminder   36
Some of the better service providers   37

Chapter 4
How to get online   **39**

PC users   42
Mac users   42
Amiga users   43
Atari ST users   43
Acorn users   44

Chapter 5
E-mail   **45**

What is e-mail?   46
What's in an e-mail address?   48
For the terminally lazy...   51
Fetch me some files, boy   52
Graphical e-mail? Whatever next?   53
And finally...   54
.net recommends   54

Chapter 6
Usenet and newsgroups   **57**

Little shop of horrors   61
UU looking at me?   61
Netiquette   62

Smileys   64
TLAs and ETLAs   64
.net recommends   65

Chapter 7
Finding stuff   **67**

FTP and Gopher   68
Where do you want to go?   71
Tell me about this Gopher business   72
We recommend...   77

Chapter 8
The World Wide Web   **79**

The Web in action   82
Getting going   84
Accessing newsgroups with a Web browser   85
Accessing FTP and Gopher with a Web browser   86
But my computer can't display pictures!   86
Run that jargon by me again   87
Software ahoy!   88
.net recommends   89

Chapter 9
HTML   **91**

What is hypertext?   93
Creating your own Web pages   94

JavaOne Chapter 10
Sun's Worldwide Java Developer Conference
Java **97**

What is it all about? 98
What is Java? 100
Java in action 101
What's in it for me? 102
Jargon killed 103

Chapter 11
Internet Relay Chat **105**

And it works like this... 107
Bored of that already? 108
Service with a smile 109
I command you to obey 110
Come chat with me 112
Chatting software here 113
What about the Web? 114

Chapter 12
Telnet **115**

Telnet for PC users 118
Telnet for Mac users 119
Try one of these... 120
.net recommends 123

Chapter 13
Future Publishing and the Internet 125

Registering for FutureNet	127
FutureNet World News	127
The Internet	127
Computing	128
Videogames	128
Sport	128
Entertainment	128
Music	129
Crafts	129
Security	129

Chapter 14
The future of the Internet 131

Index   135

Subscription offer   143

Chapter 1

Introduction

Why do you want to get on-line?

Cleverly, you have so far avoided succumbing to the hype about the Internet. Every Web address that you've seen on adverts has happily passed you by. Every Internet magazine currently groaning on the shelves of WH Smith has merrily failed to grasp your interest. Every computer manufacturer proudly boasting 'Internet compatibility' has so far failed to siphon the pounds from your pocket. So far, it would seem, so good.

But suddenly you have found yourself getting sucked into the Net's web (if you'll excuse the expression) and you aren't quite sure why. The desire to get e-mail seems strangely less resistible than it was before. Newspapers whose cynical opinions you have relied on in the past have jumped on the on-line bandwagon with haste that seems especially indecent when you consider that little less than two years ago, the majority of the country had never even heard of the term 'Internet'.

Like the first buyers of the TV or video

recorder, you know that there must be something to it but you aren't exactly sure what.
Never fear, because this book is here to tell you
exactly what. Hopefully, by the time you have
finished reading this, you'll either have thrown it
away, convinced that your suspicions were right,
and that the whole enterprise is just too worth-
less for words, or the little glimmer of interest
lurking at the back of your mind will have been
coaxed out a little into the bright on-line world.

Up until about two years ago, nobody out-
side of a few universities and computer companies had much of an idea about Internets. Then
suddenly, within the space of a couple of
months, the Internet was all over the newspapers, TV, magazines and radio programmes. And
far from that interest subsiding, as one or two
media commentators thought would happen,
the Internet has solidified its position to the
extent that it is no longer regarded as a flash in
the media pan, but a real, live new phenomenon
that is here to stay, be regulated, tamed and sold
to you by the likes of Microsoft.

Despite all this, nobody is still really sure what
the Net is, or is for. For some – people who like
their benefits hard and immediate – this has
tended to put them off. You will come across
these people at large corporations, and they will
often be the same sort of people who couldn't
see the point of getting PCs when there was a
perfectly good mainframe to use instead.

Then there are those with livelier imagina-
tions, who although unsure about what the benefits of the Net are, have put themselves on-line
anyway mainly out of a sense of exploration and,
who after the initial fun, have started to find
ways to use it productively. It is this second
group of explorers that this book is for. We'll help

you get on-line, find your way around and point
out some of the more interesting and useful
aspects of the Internet, so that whatever reasons
you eventually end up using the Net for, this
book will have shown you the way to do it.

Why are you telling me this?

The funny thing about books that explain how to
use the Internet is that they always start off by
giving you an impromptu sermon on the history
of this network of computer networks.
Unfortunately for you if you don't like history,
there is a certain amount of mileage to be had
out of explaining the Net's roots. It can help you
make sense of those annoying times when your
e-mail has taken five days to arrive, the Web site
you've been accessing for weeks suddenly
decides not to work, and there seems to be a
bunch of high-and-mighty Internet users who
heap scorn and ridicule on you when you make
even the slightest mistake. Just as you can trace
the origins of the troubles in Northern Ireland
through the sands of time, so you can track the
development of the Net and come to understand
what makes it tick.

The chances are that you've heard something
about the information superhighway and you've
picked up some nonsense about cyberspace, and
it's also more than likely that no-one will have
come up with a practical explanation of what it
all means to you. The Internet, a global network
of computer networks, is where all that media
hype and William Gibsonesque sci-fi nonsense
becomes reality. If the Net doesn't change your
life, it will certainly change the way you use your
computer. This book is all about how you can get
on-line at home.

Where has it come from?

The Internet started at the end of the 1960s, when the US military came over all twitchingly paranoid and realised that its computing systems could be wiped out by a nuclear attack by those sneaky Russkies. Working with university computer boffins across the States, the US Defense Department came up with the idea of a computer network that would be able to withstand an attack – if one part of the network went down, information would magically find its way around the damaged part and communications lines would be secure. This beast became known as the ARPANET (Advanced Research Projects Agency Network).

The magic thing about the ARPANET was that it used peer-to-peer networking, which means that the computers on the network are responsible for addressing and checking communications, rather than the network itself. In effect, this meant that if one of the computers got nuked, the information would still be able to get to its destination – it would just have to go via a different route. And rather than a computer operator telling the computers how to re-route this information, they would be able to decide how to do it themselves.

The computer data that was sent over the ARPANET was bundled up into standard packages call Internet Protocol (IP) packets, each of which contains information about the address of the destination computer.

The UNIX operating system, which came to be used in thousands of academic institutions during the 1970s and '80s, has IP networking built in, and that meant that it was easy for the academics to link into the ARPANET. Soon, it became the plaything of the university computer experts because they knew more about the networking technology than the military bigwigs who were notionally in charge of it. In this way, even networks that had been built up separately from ARPANET were eventually connected into it, hence the term 'Internet' or 'Interconnected Network of Networks.'

In the late 1980s, the US government's National Science Foundation (NSF) set up five massive supercomputer centres which users had to be able to access from anywhere in the country. The ARPANET initially provided the means of connecting them (and tens of thousands of users) together, but the bureaucracy became overbearing and the NSF decided to create its own network, NSFNET, which used the same IP technology as ARPANET. The system took off in a big way, and after some serious hardware upgrading (of both computers and telephone lines) in the late 1980s, the network was opened up to commercial traffic in the early 1990s.

It was about this time that the Internet as we know it today came into being as a network of computer networks, all of which had agreed to speak the same language, a thing called TCP/IP (Transmission Control Protocol/Internet Protocol) which you can now install on your IBM-compatible PC, Apple Mac, Amiga, ST or Acorn Archimedes. But this was only one part of the story. While the infrastructure was finally all there, something else was needed – and that was useful software. The rather limited tools that had existed up until recently might have been fine for scientific geniuses and designers of military hardware but something more was needed for the Net to take off in a mass-market kind of way.

You can find out more about the development of specific Internet tools such as the World Wide Web, Usenet discussion groups and Internet Relay Chat later in the book.

Who's in charge?

Well, no-one really. But then again, lots of people. Notionally, the Internet Society is in charge of ratifying the technological standards that make up the Net's technology, so if there's a new version of TCP/IP or HTML (HyperText Mark-up Language – more on this later) to release, it's the Internet Society that will do it.

But then the Internet Society doesn't actually control the Net, for the same reason that the Post Office doesn't run the country just because it's responsible for delivering the Prime Minister's letters.

Maybe the person who's in charge is the person who owns the Net, but then nobody really owns the Internet because it's made up of lots of individual computer networks joined together. Every bit of the Internet is owned by somebody, whether it's a government, university, company or individual, but nobody owns it all.

The companies or governments that own the high-speed backbone links probably own the most important parts, but what use is a high-speed backbone if you've got no limbs hanging off it (so to speak)?

Then again, perhaps the Government is in charge – after all, the folks in the Commons make the law of the land, so they must make the laws that govern what's on the Net, right? Not quite. The Internet is a global network, so there's no way one country's government can control what goes on it, although some have tried, and are still trying. Short of severing every phone-line into the country and knackering every mobile phone, there is no way the Government can stop Joe or Jolene Public downloading information, pictures, sound files or video clips from the Internet. Legal data on a computer in California might well be deemed illegal when it gets to Croydon, but how can the Government stop the information being transferred? It can't, and it will have a pretty tough job finding out what's on that machine in Croydon, too.

However, that's not to say several countries are trying. The US Congress recently passed what many in the on-line community regard as an insidious piece of legislation, the Communications Decency Act. This makes it a Federal offence for people to supply pornographic and other distasteful material over computer networks. Various groups in the United States are up in arms about it, because it allegedly violates Constitutional rights to free speech.

Problems have also recently been reported in Germany where the on-line service provider CompuServe recently had to pull access to the alt.sex newsgroups on Usenet (see the chapter on Newsgroups for more information) due to the allegedly illegal material freely available. And Singapore is working on ways to provide Internet access which doesn't allow illegal material into the City-State.

However, many Internet experts doubt that any of these attempts will work in the long term. The Net was designed to route information around blockages – whether blockages caused by nuclear attack or censorship – and it has to be doubtful whether any of these attempts will succeed. No doubt there's much more to be heard on these subjects in the future.

What does that mean to me?

That's just about all there is to the history of the Net. It's steeped in academia, which explains the desire for free flow of ideas and the often aggressive attitude to commercial uses of the Net. It's run and populated by computer experts, which explains why many clueless (and hapless) newcomers get a roasting when they ask for advice in the wrong places or in the wrong way. It's made up of lots of separate computer networks, so if someone switches off their computer the rest of the Net carries on working.

It existed for years without any commercial interests, so there's a great community spirit – programmers give away software for free, people make information available for nothing, and there are always people around to help. Pretty much anything goes in the discussion groups because the Net has never been controlled by anyone. However, it is now coming in for closer scrutiny from libel lawyers, obscenity detectives and worried governments, so some caution is advisable.

Blimey, whatever next?

As you might have noticed, the last couple of years have seen a massive explosion of interest in the Internet. From e-mail addresses for Children's BBC to preposterous information superhighway visuals on the News at Ten, the Net is here to stay. Part of the reason for the Net's rapid growth over recent years is the general upsurge in sales of personal computers for use in the home, the development of the World Wide Web, and a marked improvement in Internet access.

Now we've got to the stage where, thanks to

the point-and-click beauty of the World Wide Web, the Internet is almost easy to use. Anyone who is familiar with the Windows interface or an Apple Macintosh can now navigate the Net with ease. More and more companies are realising that there's money to be made from this on-line business, so the number of Internet access providers has grown to over 60 in the UK alone. What's more, they're working hard to make sure their Internet access software is easy to install and their Web and e-mail programs are easy to use.

Over the next few years there'll be an all-round improvement in Internet access. New and bigger service providers will enter the fray, with joint ventures with telecommunications companies driving the cost of access down and the speed of access up.

On-line services such as CompuServe, UK OnLine and The Microsoft Network will offer access to the Net as well as value-added information services. There'll also be more commercial Internet software. At the moment, many of the best programs are shareware or freeware, but cobbling together a suite of Net applications doesn't suit computer users who are used to buying programs off the shelf. Microsoft, IBM, Netscape, Quarterdeck and many other companies will soon be selling Internet software.

And the Net itself will soon offer much more quality information that it does now, designed for casual users, by companies like Future Publishing (publishers of this book). Perhaps one day, people will get their daily paper or magazine downloaded to them via the Net onto their TVs – it's only one in a vast galaxy of possibilities

But enough of the future, let's find out how you can get on the Internet now (or at least in five minutes' time when you've had a chance to put the kettle on).

The History of the Internet

Something old, something new... the Internet has been around for longer than you would think, although its high popularity is a new phenomenon.

- 1969 – ARPAnet commissioned by US Dept. of Defense.
- 1971 – 15 hosts, including universities, government research outfits and NASA, on ARPAnet.
- 1972 – Invention of e-mail. InterNetworking group created, chaired by Vint Cerf, which looks into establishing common standards for linking different nets.
- 1973 – UK and Norway become first international connectors to ARPAnet.
- 1974 – Vint Cerf and Bob Kahn publish their specs for linking together rival networks into an 'internet'.
- 1976 – UUCP protocol invented by Bell Labs.
- 1979 – Invention of Usenet. First multi-user dungeon game invented at Essex University.
- 1981 – Creation of BITNET and CSNET in USA. France's MINITEL goes online.
- 1982 – EUnet created in Europe. The term 'Internet' first applied to collection of Nets using the TCP/IP protocol to link together.
- 1983 – FidoNet created.
- 1984 – JANET created in UK.
- 1986 – NSFNET created to link five US super-computer sites. NNTP created to help Usenet.
- 1988 – Internet Worm crashes the Internet
- 1989 – First connection of Compuserve e-mail to Internet.
- 1990 – ARPAnet ceases to exist.

- 1991 – WAIS invented to help search Net. Gopher first released.
- 1992 – World Wide Web invented by CERN.
- 1993 – White House goes online. First MBONE broadcast.
- 1994 – Canter and Siegel spam Usenet with an advert.
- 1995 – Netscape floats on New York Stock market. Valued at over $2 billion.

Chapter 2

Choosing a modem

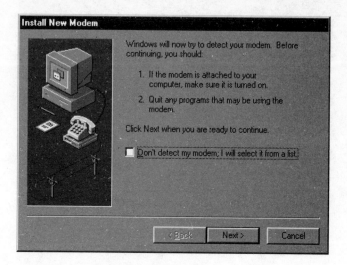

What's all this about?

Until the Internet took off, most computer magazines steered well clear of the complexities of online communications. The jargon and technical mystery associated with modems was probably part of the reason. But thanks to the Net, all of a sudden comms appears to be cool. Everyone and his dog wants to connect to the Internet, and to make the most of what's on offer, you need a decent, reliable modem.

The good news is that modem prices, as with the cost of all hardware, have been falling. Modem manufacturers such as Motorola and Pace are making an effort to cater for Internet-hungry computer users by producing special 'get on the Net' bundles, which include a modem and all the software you need to, er, 'get on the Net.'

All a modem (derived from the term

'MOdulater DEModulater') does is convert the digital signals produced by your computer into audio ones that can be sent down a telephone line. The modem at the other end of the line converts the signal back into a form the computer can understand, and hey presto! You've sent a file round the corner, or halfway round the world, without seeing hide nor hair of a floppy disk or a Federal Express parcel. Nowadays, you can even send faxes from your PC, or have a combined modem/fax/answering machine all in one box.

It isn't quite as simple as just buying a modem and plugging it in, however – you have to make sure you have the right features, the right standards, and the right software.

If you intend to connect your modem to BT's telephone network, you should buy one that has BABT (British Approvals Board for Telecommunications) approval – it should have a little green circle on it somewhere.

If you connect a modem that isn't BABT approved to the BT network, you're breaking the law. BABT-approved modems are likely to have better design and components than non-approved modems (which have to display large red triangle stickers to show their unworthiness) and they're also more likely to come from solid, reputable companies.

In the past, approved modems were significantly more expensive than non-approved ones, but increasing competition in the modem market has brought prices down significantly. For example, the Pace MobiFax is a BABT-approved fax/modem that only costs around £99, so it really isn't worth scrimping to save a few pennies when quality products are available at such low prices.

That was a bit heavy...

The next thing you have to consider is so obvious it isn't obvious at all – where are you going
to put your modem? If you've got several acres
of free desk space or a tiny slim-line PC case with
no free expansion slots, you're going to need an
external modem. Those of you with hulking
great floor-standing tower systems, that need
planning permission before they're erected, will
have enough spare slots to house several small
refugee families as well as an internal modem
card. The choice is yours, and there's not much
difference in price. Mac, Amiga, ST and
Archimedes users will only be able to choose an
external model. Whatever your type of computer,
if you plump for an external model, make sure
the modem is supplied with the right cable to
connect it to your machine. If it's not, nip down
to your nearest friendly computer shop and
buy one.

If you're at all wary of opening up your PC to
fit expansion cards, then steer clear of internal
modems because they can be harder to set up
than their external brethren. Any difficulties are
normally limited to finding an available interrupt,
but this can be incredibly frustrating if you aren't
a technical boffin. Windows – and a number of
other Microsoft packages – comes with a DOS
utility called MSD, which has a stab at telling you
which interrupts are free. Another internal option
to consider for a PC is the PCMCIA modem card,
which is probably of most interest if you own a
portable PC. Don't worry if yours is one of the
millions of PCs that doesn't have an PCMCIA slot,
Psion Dacom has launched an 8-bit ISA half card
into which you can insert a PCMCIA modem.
The card costs £50 in conjunction with one of

Psion's Gold Card modems (which cost £219 and upwards), or £99 on its own.

How fast a modem you need depends on how you intend to use it. The faster the modem, the less time you'll spend racking up phone bills while sending and receiving data. That's a real boon in these wonderful days of multimedia, as you're just as likely to be downloading sound and picture files as you are to be sending text, but the catch is that the faster a modem is, the more it costs to buy. Speed is measured in baud rate, which is roughly equivalent to how many bits the modem can send per second, although modern modems can send more than one bit of information at a time, increasing the speed considerably.

Look at the numbers in a modem's specification, and you'll see several V numbers – V22, V22bis, V32 and so on – which are standards set by the CCITT (Comité Consultatif International Téléphonique et Télégraphique, an international standards body). Most of these numbers describe how many bits per second (bps) a modem can send or receive, but just to confuse matters, some refer to error checking and data compression capabilities. The most important ones to be aware of are these:

V22 – 1,200bps (about 120 characters a second)
V22bis – an improved version of V22 at
          2,400bps, supported by nearly all
          modems and services
V32 – 9,600bps
V32bis – 14,400bps
V34 – 28,000bps
V42 – an error checking standard
V42bis – a data compression standard

After V32bis, you get into the murky waters
so often found in the PC world of non-standard
standards. V32 Terbo and V.Fast Class are faster V
numbers still – 28,000bps – but are not official
CCITT standards. V42 is an official standard for
error correction which improves your chance of
sending data over a bad line. The data is rigor-
ously checked as it is received to ensure it match-
es the data that was sent. This inevitably slows
down transfer time, so if you want to eke out
some extra speed from your V32bis modem
that's using V42 error checking, the standard to
watch for is V42bis which uses data compression
at both ends of the line to reduce the time it
takes to send the data.

So which one should I buy?

Nowadays, you probably won't find a modem
running at less than 2,400bps, but if you're
going to be using the Internet, look for a bps of
at least 14,400, and if you've got another £100
knocking around, consider plumping for a
28,800bps model. A good mid-range 14,400bps
option is the US Robotics Sportster – see below –
while at the top end of the modem scale, the
28,800bps Sonix Volante Fast reigns supreme,
but then again it should do – its RRP is only a
fiver under £800. If you're going to be a heavy
user (exploring the Internet and downloading
files can soon become a frighteningly addictive
and time-consuming hobby), it won't be long
before you've recouped the extra outlay by
reducing the time you've spent on-line racking
up your phone bill. Remember, you don't just
pay for the phone call, with many commercial
systems such as CompuServe you pay for the
amount of time you spend logged on to certain

areas of the system so a good rule of thumb is: always go for the fastest modem you can afford.

Before you plump for that super-fast 28,800 baud beast, check which speeds are offered by the services you intend to use. CIX and CompuServe only offer 14,400 baud access at the moment, so there's no point getting a faster modem if you're just using them. If, on the other hand, you've got a friend across the Atlantic with whom you regularly exchange files, it could well be worth both of you investing in one of the faster models.

Many Internet service providers are upgrading their Internet access nodes (called points of presence or PoPs) to 28,800bps, making it worth splashing out £100 extra because you'll be able to cut your phone bill.

By this stage, you've probably focused in on roughly the speed and sort of modem you want, and now it's a matter of weighing up the ease of use and extra options provided by each modem. External modems are generally easier to set up, and often have status lights to tell you what the modem's up to – not essential by any means, but a good feature if it doesn't cost any extra. If you're going to be working from home, a fax/modem will probably be a good buy and nearly all modems now come with built-in fax. This means you'll be able to send faxes from your PC without having to print the document first. Faxes can also be sent to your PC and displayed in bitmap form on the screen, and if your fax software has optical character recognition you can get the text out as a text file.

It's currently impossible to find a low-cost modem that combines decent functionality with the ease of use normally associated with consumer products. When choosing and using a modem for the first-time, it is important to examine which software and manuals are provided. If there is no communications software supplied, you'll have to spend extra money on a commercial comms package, or try to find a shareware equivalent – either way it's extra hassle that you could do without.

Most modems are supplied with basic Windows and Macintosh comms and fax software. Other welcome extras are programs which give you limited trial access to on-line systems such as CompuServe, so you can see if cruising the network is to your liking before you take out a subscription. Many modems are now supplied with trial Internet accounts as well.

We recommend...

14,400bps modems

• MobiFax 144
£99, Pace, ☎ 01274 532000
A portable modem which works just as well as its Microlin sister, which costs £199.

• Sportster 14,400
£139, US Robotics, ☎ 0800 225252
An excellent 14,400bps external modem that offers a wide range of features at a sensible price. The equivalent version for the Mac is called the Mac 'n' Fax.

• Tornado 14,400 Fax/Modem
£104.57, Future Publishing, ☎ 01225 822511
A great, low-cost, but well-featured modem that's ideal if you are just starting out in the on-line world.

28,800 modems

• Express 28.8E Fax Modem
£217.38, (PC) £240.68 (Mac), Express
Technology, ☎ 01784 421123
A smart high-performance modem with excellent
features and an effective design. And it's cheap.

• Linnet 34 fx
£352.53, Pace, ☎ 01274 532000
A well-featured beast with easily accessible ports
on the rear and a clear display on the front.

• Power PK-2880M
£210.33, Gasteiner, ☎ 0181 345 6000
A tiny beast this one, but what power it packs
into its little body. Easy to install, portable and
available for both Mac and PC.

• Sportster 28,800
£199, US Robotics, ☎ 0800 225252
It's fab.

• Tornado FM288E
£189.29, Future Publishing, ☎ 01225 822511
An ugly little beggar, but boy is it fast – and
cheap.

Chapter 3

Choosing a Net Service Provider

Whether you want to get on-line at work, school, university or home, all the hardware you need to get on the Net is a computer, a modem and a phone line. Then you just have to arrange for someone to give (or rather, sell) you a connection to the Net, which is what an Internet service provider will do. In effect, these companies are selling you your way into the Net. More than 60 of them have sprung up in the UK over the last two years and here's how you can decide to choose one.

Work out where you are

You'll often hear Internet pundits saying that one of the great things about the Net is that you can access computers on the other side of the world for the cost of a local phone call. This is only the case if your Internet service provide has an access node (usually called a point of presence or PoP) within a local telephone call from your computer. If you live in Torquay, there's no point choosing a service provider that only has a point of presence in the Outer Hebrides because every time you log on to the Net you'll be making a long-distance phone call.

Many of the smaller service providers were set up to serve specific regions, for example the Brighton area is well served by Pavilion and the Shetlands by Zetnet. The larger service providers such as Unipalm Pipex and Demon have entered into agreements with telephone companies (Mercury and Energis respectively) to provide points of presence across the whole country which means that even if the company is located in London, you still should be able to access the Net for the cost of a local call.

There we go then: choose a service provider that has a point of presence within range of a local telephone call. Better still, if you're a customer of a cable telephone company, choose a service provider that is also a customer of said company so your local call to log on to the Internet will be absolutely free.

What do you want to do with it?

Bit of a chicken-and-egg kind of question this one. You won't know exactly which bits of the Net you'll use most until you're actually on-line, but you can't choose the best type of account without knowing which bits of the Net you're going to use most. It is with a heavy heart that we splice said chicken asunder and crack the egg into the Frying Pan of Eternity and tell you this.

You want to send e-mail (and lots of it). You want to use the World Wide Web, which is the sexy multimedia hip 'n' trendy easy-to-use part of the Net. You want to access the 13,000 subject-based Usenet discussion groups (called newsgroups) and take part in arguments about whether the continuity error in Pulp Fiction when

Vincent Vegas claims to never have watched television and then later laughs at Jules' TV-related joke is important. To do all of this (and quite a lot more) you need a regular account with a regular Internet service provider. You should expect to pay a set-up fee of between £25 and £50, and then a flat-rate monthly fee of £10 to £20. The only other charge you then have is your phone bill.

The alternative is to choose to get on-line through a commercial service such as CompuServe, CIX or UK OnLine. These have the advantage of information and chat areas which can only be accessed by subscribers to the service and have simple software, but they only offer restricted access to the Internet, for example CIX currently doesn't offer World Wide Web access. Also, these services charge for every single second you are logged on to the system, which can make cruising the World Wide Web a very expensive business.

If you're a complete technophobe (and rather rich to boot), it might be worth considering accessing the Net through CompuServe, but many Internet service providers are now offering easy-to-install software which dulls CompuServe's competitive edge. Take our advice, go for a regular service provider.

What about software?

When you set up an account with a service provider, you'll be sent a disk or three in the post. Until recently, Internet software was a pig to install, but the providers have got their collective act together and are now supplying installation programs that can get you on-line with the click of a button. .net regularly does random spot-checks of the software supplied by service providers, and Bogomip, Unipalm Pipex and CityScape are pretty much at the top of the pile when it comes to Mac and Windows. But it's not just the installation routine that's important, you need to make sure that you're supplied with basic Net access software.

As a bare minimum you should expect a World Wide Web browser (Netscape Navigator or a version of Mosaic is most likely), an e-mail program (Eudora and Mail-It are common and very good), a newsreader for reading newsgroups and an FTP program for downloading files. It's not desperate if any of these aren't supplied because you can always download more programs from the Net, but when you're starting out you need as much help as you can get and having all the software you need supplied on a disk is a boon.

And the modem at the other end?

Remember when we were having that quiet chat about modems, and we glibly commented "Before you plump for that super-fast 28,800 baud beast, check which speeds are offered by the services you intend to use."? Well, we're going to say it again, only the other way round. If you've got a 28,800bps modem, it's worth finding a service provider that offers 28,800bps Net access.

Unipalm Pipex has recently upgraded all of its points of presence, and CompuServe and Demon aim to do the same in the near future. If your choice of service provider is restricted to two or three choices in your local region who only offer 14,400bps access, ask them whether they plan to upgrade to 28,800bps and pick the one that gives the most convincing reply.

While you're on the phone, you could do a lot worse than ask about the service provider's user to modem ratio. Service providers have to install modems in all their points of presence, and the user to modem ratio tells you how many customers will be battling to get on the Net through those modems. A ratio of around 15:1 is acceptable. Demon has come in for a lot of criticism because it became a victim of its own success. Not surprisingly, its low monthly charge of £10+VAT attracted a good few thousand customers, which meant it didn't have enough modems to cope with demand. It took some frustrated customers days to download their e-mail and accessing Demon's newsgroups was once a non-starter. Demon's recent expansion has largely solved the problem, but as with all fables, there is a lesson to be learned and it is this: it can be false economy to go for the cheapest option.

How will you be paying?

Many service providers require that you pay by credit card a month in advance or by direct debit, and some don't even take cheques. Basically you're stuffed if you haven't got a bank account, so get one. That's just all about you need to know, service provider-wise. For the latest details of UK providers, check out the full list that's updated and printed every month in .net.

A reminder

1) Find a service provider which has a PoP near to where you live, so you can dial into the Internet for the cost of a local call. Most service providers now aim to have this facility.

2) Decide how much you want to spend. Generally, you pay for speed and quality, and particularly for connections through big players like CompuServe.

3) Decide what level of access you want – some providers restrict access to certain parts of the Internet.

4) Make sure the service provider supports connections at least at 14,400 bps.

5) Make sure the service provider supplies you with all the relevant software.

6) Make sure there's an after-sales service. When you first connect, it's likely you will have some problems getting everything to work properly.

7) Finally, make sure the company supports the make of computer you use! Some companies support the Macintosh, some do not – phone first and be sure.

Some of the better service providers

All these companies keep their pricing under review – please call them to get the latest pricing information and local Point-of-Presence availability.

• Atlas, ☎ 0171 312 0400
£30 set-up charge, £14 per month.

• Bogomip, ☎ 0800 137536
£25 set-up charge (£50 for home installation/tutorial). £12 per month.

- CityScape Internet Services, ☎ 01223 566950
£180 to £1000 per annum.

- CIX (Limited Internet Access), ☎ 0181 390 6561
£25 set-up charge. Hourly rates.

- CompuServe, ☎ 0800 289378
(All prices are US$): $10 a month, $4.80 per hour. Extra rates for premium services.

- Demon Internet Limited, ☎ 0181 371 1234
£15 set-up, £12 per month.

- Easynet, ☎ 0171 209 0990
£25 set-up, £12 per month

- IBM, ☎ 01926 464167
£10 per month for three hours

- netkonect, ☎ 0171 345 777
£10 per month for basic service

- Pavilion Internet, ☎ 01273 607072
£18 set-up, £15-£18 per month

- RedNet Limited, ☎ 01494 513333
£25 set-up, £15 per month

- Unipalm Pipex, ☎ 01223 250120
£180 per annum +

Chapter 4

How to get online

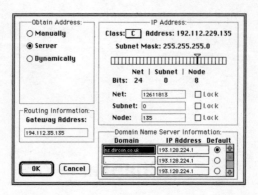

Putting your computer on the Net is getting easier by the month as Internet service providers improve their installation software. Here's an overview of what you need to do to get on-line (please check with your service providers for exact details – some providers use different software to others – and some don't support certain computers at all.)

1. Buy a computer. A PC or Mac is ideal because these machines have the most software support, but you can get on-line with an Acorn computer, Amiga or Atari ST. If you're getting on the Net from home, it's unlikely that you'll be using UNIX, so we'll ignore that from now.

2. Choose a modem – many PCs are sold equipped with modems these days.

3. Choose an Internet service provider (see appropriate chapter).

4. It's also a good idea at this point to sort out your relevant details:

(a) your made-up domain name: some providers provide Net access in a slightly more flexible ways than others. For instance, Demon allow you to choose a 'domain name' which is just a fancy way of letting you run more than one e-mail address. You can see the advantage to this if you ran your own business – call your domain something like 'supacleen.demon.co.uk' (you have to include the 'Demon' bit because that's who's providing you Net access) and run e-mail addresses of it for sales@supacleen.demon.co.uk, invoicing@supacleen.demon.co.uk, or boss@supacleen.demon.co.uk. You get the idea.

(b) Your e-mail address – witty or practical.

(c) Your method of payment (most providers can bill directly to your credit card): remember that service providers charge you on a monthly basis, in much the same way as mobile phone operators do.

(d) …And any other extras you need. If in doubt, phone the provider. Some service providers give you a default e-mail address to start off with and then give you the chance to create aliases for it at your leisure.

5. Contact the provider and ask it to set up an account. It'll prompt you for the relevant details, and, depending on the provider, your account should be set up within a few hours of the phone call. Make sure you state what sort of computer you're using because this will determine what software it sends you.

6. Find the point of presence nearest to you – your provider can provide a list. Demon and

Pipex currently have PoPs all around the country, so even if their main office is in London, there should be a local connection near you (which obviously will save you loads of money on your phone bills).

7. Set up the software the provider gives you – this may be more complicated than it sounds. Demon, for instance, pretty much leaves it up to you, although it has a new easy-to-install system due out soon. CityScape, Pipex and Bogomip, on the other hand, are a lot friendlier. Either way, the chances are that you will have to phone the servicer provider at least once, so make sure that technical support is provided.

PC users

Much of the software now supplied by Internet service providers comes with everything you need to get your PC on-line, including the fabled TCP/IP nonsense and an arcane piece of file trickery called WINSOCK.DLL. There is absolutely no reason for you to have to scrabble about patching together a makeshift system in this way – the provider should do all the work for you. If it doesn't, get your money back and go elsewhere.

Mac users

Get hold of the control panel MacTCP. MacTCP is commercial software from Apple – some service providers have a licence to distribute it, others don't. If you open a CityScape account you'll automatically get a copy from them. Otherwise buy either The Mac Internet Starter Kit by Adam Engst or The Mac Internet Tour Guide by Michael Fraase, both of which include a copy of MacTCP on their software disk (the books are useful too). Follow the instructions from your service provider to configure your account via the ConfigPPP and MacTCP control panels. If you are luckier and own a newer Mac with Sytem 7.5, you already have MacTCP.

Amiga users
Unlike other computers, all Net software for the Amiga is free, thanks to a great bunch of people at the University of Helsinki in Finland. Unfortunately, because the Amiga is declining in popularity, support from the service providers can be patchy at best. The TCP/IP networking software, AmiTCP, is freely available from any Aminet site (such as the COMM/NET directory of FTP.DOC.AC.IC.UK). Unfortunately, it's a pain to set up – although Demon Internet has written its own installation software, which sorts out a lot of the more painful stuff for you. All you need to do is provide your details and IP address and the program does the rest. It even installs a special SLIP driver which automatically handles dialling out on the modem and connecting to the Net.

However, if you're using another service provider, you'll have to install AmiTCP yourself. Included with the latest version of the software are all of the network tools you'll need, including FTP, Telnet and Archie. But bear in mind that most of the really current Net software is only really supported by the Mac and PC.

Atari ST users
A decent ST set-up is important – a minimum of 2Mb of RAM and a hard drive is essential. Stuart Coates (scoates@filesys.demon.co.uk) has compiled all the software you need into one self-extracting archive called ATARINOS.TOS for Demon Internet. Demon can supply you with a Bulletin Board number which will enable you to

download the file using normal communications software. Demon Internet is providing ST connection software, call 0181 349 0063. The kit supplied consists of TCP/IP software KA9Q, e-mail software, Usenet software, finger, Telnet, and an FTP program. Everything is ported across from DOS PC versions, so there is a distinct lack of GEM.

Acorn users

The Archimedes has been rather neglected with regards to the Internet. Until quite recently, the only way you could get on-line was with a trusty old comms package such as ArcTerm7 or Hearsay II. Acorn users will need to get hold of either the !TCPIP v2.01 TCP/IP protocol and Internet applications suite, or Slipdial v0.32 which is pre-set to access Demon. Web browsers such as ArcWeb and Webster are now available. Call Demon or Acorn for more assistance.

8. Log on. If everything's gone well you should be prompted for a password and given other salient details.

9. If you find the provided software isn't quite up to scratch, there are plenty of FTP sites on the Net which provide alternatives. Get searching! Just nip along to http://www.yahoo.com/ and do a search there for the latest sites.

Chapter 5

E-mail

Computer users can be a cynical bunch and who's to blame them? As soon as a user has forked out for the latest hyped bit of equipment, something else seems to slide along right behind it, making that original considered and hard-won decision look a little out of date.

So it's hardly a surprise that many have tended to regard the Net as little more than a passing fad but this attitude risks overlooking the one solid, honest and clear benefit of joining the Internet – electronic mail.

Many people will be familiar with e-mail from their jobs – and many people will possibly be familiar with Internet e-mail from their jobs too. But before we go any further into this, let's explain exactly what it is that we are talking about.

What is e-mail?

E-mail comes in two forms. The form most people are familiar with is the kind that is used inter-

nally at your job. Then there's Internet e-mail.
Both do the same things, although slightly differently. But as far as the user is concerned the dif-
ferences are disappearing as many companies
have now hooked their office e-mail into the
Internet. This means it's now possible for small
companies to benefit from a global e-mail system, something only huge multinationals were
able to afford.

But personal users can benefit as well. Some
emigre families now use e-mail to keep in touch
with each other (it's cheaper than the phone and
faster than the post – and you can 'talk' daily if
you like), and Internet e-mail has been used
widely to alert the World to natural disasters, like
the Kobe earthquake in Japan.

So e-mail is simply a way of sending text
messages to other people who have Internet
access. It's a bit like a using fax machine, only
without the funny glossy paper, or the engaged
tone on the machine at the other end, or the
need to print out your message once you've
typed it in.

In fact, it's nothing like using a fax machine
because you can e-mail several thousand people
at the touch of one button, do groovy things like
access World Wide Web pages, and even join discussion groups that bombard you with messages
without you having to lift a finger. E-mail is fast
(messages can be delivered to the other side of
the world in less than five minutes – although
equally, it can sometimes take three days), it's
cheap (the cost of a local phone call no matter
where you're sending it), and it's also one of the
most efficient ways of communicating in this
electronic day and age.

When you open an account with an Internet
provider, it normally provides an e-mail address

as standard (if it doesn't go elsewhere!). There
are a couple of different types of e-mail accounts,
SMTP (Simple Mail Transfer Protocol) and POP3
(Post Office Protocol 3). The former is an older
type of e-mail system used to transfer messages
over the Internet, POP3 mail is a newer and more
efficient system for doing the exactly the same
thing. Both systems store your mail for you on
your service provider's machine until you log on
to the system. With SMTP you have to use a program to request that the messages are downloaded to your PC, but with a POP3 account this
happens automatically.

What's in an e-mail address?

When you set up an account with an Internet
service provider you'll be given an e-mail
address, or you might be able to choose your
own. E-mail addresses can look confusing, but
they're easy to understand when you know what
all the parts mean. My e-mail address is nmer-
ritt@futurenet.co.uk and here's what it means,
starting with the part after the @ (which is
known as the 'domain'):

uk means the domain is on a computer the
United Kingdom. Every country has a two-letter
code, known in the Internet trade as the top-
level domain code. You won't see the us code for
the USA used very often because of the following...

co means the domain belongs to a company.
Alternatives are ac for academic institutions such
as a university, gov for governmental domains
and org for organisations such as charities
(Greenpeace is at greenpeace.org, for example).

Just to make things a little more confusing, companies in the US just use com instead of co.us
and US universities use edu instead of ac.us Tsk.

futurenet is the domain name which Future
Publishing registered with the Internet Society
which approves names and hands out Internet
Protocol numbers to go with them. Every computer on the Net has an Internet Protocol (IP)
address, and the domain name is mapped on
to this.

nmerritt is my username. The Internet doesn't
know or even care how many people live in the
futurenet.co.uk domain, it just delivers messages
there and then the futurenet.co.uk mail computer delivers all the mail to the individual users.

Once you've set up your Internet account,
sorted out your e-mail address and got your e-
mail software running, it's time to send some
messages. Most e-mail programs are very easy to
use now, especially ones which run on the Mac
or in Windows. You can add people to address
books so you don't have to type in their e-mail
address every time you want to write to them,
you can click on a button to reply directly to mail
you've received, you can save messages to your
hard disk, automatically filter in-coming mail into
separate folders or directories, and even set up
automatic responses.

It's a good idea to write your e-mail message
before you connect to the Internet so you can
minimise your phone bill. You should log on to
collect your e-mail, log off, read your messages
at leisure, compose your replies and then log
back on to send them, and then log off again.
Composing your messages off-line (as this is

called) also gives you more time to think about what you're saying so you're not forced into sending hasty replies just to keep your phone bill down.

Your e-mail program will also enable you to create one or more signatures – short messages which appear at the bottom of any messages you send. Some people draw fancy ASCII art, while others just write their name and a favourite quotation. It's considered bad manners to have a signature file that's more than four lines long, because (they say) this exerts an unnecessary strain on the Net's resources and the people on the receiving end have to pay money to experience your vanity (see the Netiquette chapter later in the book for more of these unofficial rules).

When you're sending an e-mail, make sure you enter the address correctly. If you get it wrong, the mail will 'bounce back' with a message from someone's mail server telling you that the address wasn't recognised.

You're not restricted to sending text messages with e-mail. Binary files such as GIF pictures or word-processed documents can be sent as an attachment or enclosure.

A special encoding system called MIME (Multipurpose Internet Mail Extensions) does the clever stuff for you – all you have to do is select the Attach or Enclose File option from within your e-mail software (such as Eudora on the PC or Mac) and send your message. All the encoding is performed automatically, and the file is automatically decoded when it is received. It's a good idea to ask the person on the receiving end whether they're using the same software as you – it's no use sending a binary file across the Net if the recipient hasn't got a program that can use it.

For the terminally lazy...

If you want to receive stacks of e-mail, you don't have to contact hundreds of people individually, you can join a mailing list instead. A mailing list is a discussion group that sends all the messages it receives to everyone who's subscribed to that list, often on a daily basis. Mailing lists cover virtually every topic you care to think of, and plenty you'd rather not.

There are a couple of types of mailing list, some run by humans, some run by machines. The subscription address of a human list will look something like this: movies-request@movienews.com. The -request part of the address indicates that it is a manually run mailing list. To subscribe to this type of mailing list, send a polite e-mail something like:

> Please subscribe me to the movies mailing list. My full name is Nick Merritt, my e-mail address is nmerritt@futurenet.co.uk

It's considered to be good manners to include your full name in the message.

Automatic mailing lists are easy to spot because they have either majordomo or listserv in the address. Your request has to be sent in a set format because computers are stupid and easily confused. If you stray from the format in any way, your message is rejected and the machine will send you an error message.

To subscribe to .net's announcement list, send a subscribe netmag-announce message to majordomo@futurenet.co.uk Remember to leave the subject line blank and to disable your automatic signature because it would confuse the software at the other end. If you don't know what to do, you can send a help or info message to the majordomo or listserv address.

To get a full list of mailing lists, send a message to listserv@bitnic.educom.edu with the text 'list global' as the body of the message. In return you'll get a very, very large e-mail back listing all the available mailing lists world-wide. The list is divided up into more manageable alphabetical sections and regularly posted to the alt.etext and alt.zines newsgroups.

Fetch me some files, boy

The normal method of getting binary files over the Net is to use FTP, but if you don't have any FTP software, you can use something called FTP mail. All you have to do is send an e-mail message to an FTP mail server – a special system which converts binary files into a text file that can be sent to you as e-mail. The only snag is that these text files tend to be much larger than the binary originals, which means that the e-mails you receive are split into 64K chunks which have to be stitched back together again. This process is known as uuencoding (turning binary files into ASCII text) and uudecoding (turning ASCII text files back into binary).

There are a series of instructions you need to use to get a file using FTP mail – you have to know the name of the file you want to download and the address of the FTP machine that it's stored on. Here's the e-mail message you would send to get a file called CJPEG.EXE from a university machine in the US.

To: ftpmail@doc.ic.ac.uk
Subject: FTP mail

reply nmerritt@futurenet.co.uk

```
reply nmerritt@futurenet.co.uk
connect ftp.cis.nctu.edu.tw:
chdir upload/graphics
binary
uuencode
get cjpeg.exe
quit
```

For full details of all FTP mail commands, send an
e-mail to ftpmail@doc.ic.ac.uk with the text
'help' as the body text of the message. A full list
of all FTP mail commands will be e-mailed back
to you. FTP mail messages take quite a while to
process, so don't be surprised if it takes a few
days for the e-mail to arrive.

Graphical e-mail? Whatever next?

E-mail is also useful for accessing graphical parts
of the Internet such as the World Wide Web on
machines that don't have graphics capabilities.
You can get the text and graphics from a Web
page using e-mail, but you won't be able to display it as if you were using an ordinary World
Wide Web browser.

Send an e-mail to listproc@www0.cern.ch
with the letters www followed by the URL of the
Web page you want to access as the body of the
message. For example, if you want to get details
of .net's home page you would send the text:

www http://www.futurenet.co.uk/net.html

as the body of the message. This retrieves just
the text of the page. To retrieve more details
from the page, send an e-mail with the body
text:

```
connect ftp.cis.nctu.edu.tw:
chdir upload/graphics
binary
uuencode
get cjpeg.exe
quit
```

For full details of all FTP mail commands, send an e-mail to ftpmail@doc.ic.ac.uk with the text 'help' as the body text of the message. A full list of all FTP mail commands will be e-mailed back to you. FTP mail messages take quite a while to process, so don't be surprised if it takes a few days for the e-mail to arrive.

Graphical e-mail? Whatever next?

E-mail is also useful for accessing graphical parts of the Internet such as the World Wide Web on machines that don't have graphics capabilities. You can get the text and graphics from a Web page using e-mail, but you won't be able to display it as if you were using an ordinary World Wide Web browser.

Send an e-mail to listproc@www0.cern.ch with the letters www followed by the URL of the Web page you want to access as the body of the message. For example, if you want to get details of .net's home page you would send the text:

www http://www.futurenet.co.uk/net.html

as the body of the message. This retrieves just the text of the page. To retrieve more details from the page, send an e-mail with the body text:

deep http://www.futurenet.co.uk/net.html

This will get the text of page the plus all the hypertext links used in the page.

And finally...

If you want to find out more about the various ways you can use e-mail, send an e-mail message to MAILBASE@mailbase.ac.uk using the upper case letters exactly as we've shown here. Leave the subject line blank, and enter the following text as the body of the e-mail message:

send lis-iis e-access-inet.txt

After a while you'll get a message back from the mailbase telling everything you'll ever need to know about using e-mail. If you're after a shareware e-mail program, you can find the addresses of some in the directory.

There are loads of e-mail programs, but we have listed some of our favourites here. These will tend to be the ones supplied by service providers but there are also commercial ones available (which cost a lot of money). The ones listed here can be yours for nothing:

.net recommends

For the PC

• Eudora
ftp://src.doc.ic.ac.uk/pub/packages/ibmpc/
eudora/windows
Probably the best Windows e-mail program around and it's a shareware program too.

• PCElm

ftp://ftp.demon.co.uk/ibmpc/DIS/pcelm111.zip
Off-line e-mail program for DOS. It's primitive
but does the job if you don't have Windows.

For the Mac

• Eudora
http://www..qualcomm.com/quest
It's great on the PC, so there's no reason why it
shouldn't be great on the Mac. And it is.

For the Acorn

• Newsbse 0.50
ftp://mnhep1.hep.umn.edu/acorn/
Combined e-mail and Usenet newsgroup program.

For the Atari ST

• Oasis
ftp://ftp.demon.co.uk/pub/atari/oasis
Combined e-mail and news reader.

Chapter 6

Usenet and newsgroups

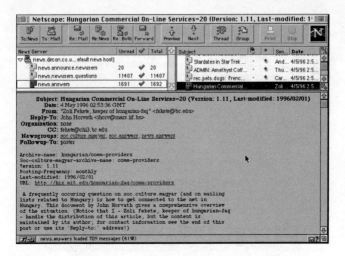

Shock! Horror! Tabloid hysteria! Much of the bad press you'll read about the Net comes from this very popular part of it. Essentially, Usenet is nothing more than a gigantic collection of discussion groups. If you have an interest, it is sure to be represented here. Each individual discussion area is called a newsgroup and they an range from the funny, to the useful, to the trivial, to the shocking (and that's where the media interest tends to enter the equation).

But the amount of hard news in the vast majority of these 13,000+ discussion areas is approximately nil. Tittletattlegroups would be a more appropriate name for the multi-megabyte discussion forum that is Usenet, but even though the chat is often trivial, it's always hugely entertaining.

To read the newsgroups, you need to be able to access a news server (these are the computers which distribute the messages sent to the newsgroups). Most major UK service providers run news servers and provide newsgroup access as a standard part of the Internet access package. The news servers (and there are hundreds of them on the Net) are set up to exchange information with the nearest machine, so when a new message is posted to one news server, it gradually gets passed across the Net from machine to machine. This means that a message that becomes immediately visible on, say, CityScape's news server, might take a couple of days to reach a news server in Sydney.

Your service provider should even provide you with a newsreader program, the software you need to read and send newsgroup messages (there's a list of the best ones at the end of this chapter). If the software doesn't come pre-configured, you'll need to tell it the address of the news server you're using, which will probably be your service provider's domain name preceded by the word news, for example news.cityscape. co.uk. Some service providers restrict access to their news server to their own customers, while others, such as Demon, allow all and sundry to log on.

There are so many newsgroups that you're bound to find something you're interested in, and plenty of things you didn't know you were interested in. Just about every major rock group has its own discussion group, for example, as does any sexual persuasion (or perversion). For this last reason, some service providers censor out some of the more appalling groups. Compuserve, for instance, due to legal action in Germany, does not allow access to the alt.sex groups but the problem here is that although some of the alt.sex groups are used to trade pornography, some are abuse survivor support groups. Demon however provides unrestricted access at time of writing.

The groups are divided into several main areas, identified by the first few letters of the newsgroup name.

alt   alternative topics (can cover anything – these tend to be the most interesting and unregulated)

comp   computer-related subjects

news   discussion about Usenet

rec   recreational topics such as sport, music and films

sci   scientific discussion

soc   cultural and social talk

uk   for topics related to the UK

To get involved in a newsgroup discussion, you first have to subscribe to the group you're interested in. With most newsreaders you simply highlight the name of the newsgroup listed in the full group list and select subscribe from the appropriate menu. When you've subscribed to a group, your newsreader will download all the messages that have been sent to that group since the last time you logged on. Most service providers delete messages after about three days, so it's a good idea to log on regularly to make sure you don't miss any of the chat.

When you have downloaded the messages, it's a good idea to disconnect from your service provider before reading them so you don't run up unnecessary phone bills. When you've composed your replies or written any new messages, you can log on again to post them to the group. When you get bored of a certain newsgroup, you can unsubscribe from it by highlighting it and selecting the appropriate command from the menu.

Little shop of horrors

When brainless media types drone on about the
sea of porn that is the Internet, they're mainly
talking about Usenet. They don't actually know
this because they're stupid, but pornography,
soft and hard, is readily available in the Usenet
newsgroups. If you're worried about your children accessing some of the alt.binaries.pictures.
erotica newsgroups, you have several choices.
Use a service provider (such as the BBC
Networking Cub) whose news server doesn't give
you access to these groups. Or you can install a
program such as Net Nanny, which shuts down
your PC as soon as a user-defined word (such as
'sex' or 'throbbing') is typed in. Alternatively,
simply raise your children to be as outraged and
disgusted by pornography as you are (a long-
term solution admittedly, but ultimately it's the
most effective).

UU looking at me?

Because of technical limitations, all Usenet post-
ings are made in 7-bit ASCII format, which
means that it's an ideal system for exchanging
text but is less than perfect for swapping binary
files such as pictures, programs, video clips and
sound samples. To send a binary file to a newsgroup you have to use a process called uuencoding, which converts the 8-bit binary file to 7-bit
ASCII. You can spot uuencoded messages on
Usenet because they look like complete gibberish
(as opposed to just reading like complete gibberish, but that's just a comment on the level of
debate on Usenet). When you've downloaded
the message, you need to convert it back into
binary by uudecoding it. The program you need

to do this is a uudecoder/uuencoder, and you can get one for most computer formats from the large FTP sites. (The Mac's one is called UUundo).

Netiquette

People are often quick to tell you that anything goes on the Net, that it's a complete anarchy and so on. They claim that there's no one to tell you what to do, that no-one's in charge and that there are no rules. These people are wrong. There is a set of foul-smelling 'unofficial' rules called Netiquette that some Net users enforce with the vigour and dedication of Judge Dredd on PCP.

These rules are nothing more than simple guidelines on how you should behave on-line, tips that should make everyone's time on the Net much more pleasant. In fact, one of the best reasons for trying to stick to them is so you don't get a mailbox full of abuse from a self-appointed Net cop, whose loud-mouthed on-line persona usually makes up for his shortfall in the trouser department in the real world. Most of these rules apply when you're posting and replying to messages in Usenet newsgroups, but many are handy hints for good e-mail practice as well.

Always read the Frequently Asked Questions file for a given newsgroup before posting messages to it. It will tell you what the group is (and isn't for) and enable you to work out whether you're asking your question or raising a subject in the appropriate area – there's nothing Net cops hate more than people posting irrelevant messages in newsgroups. The FAQ will probably be posted regularly to the group, but if you can't find it post a message in the group asking for someone to direct you to it. It will probably be held at an FTP site somewhere.

Don't send your messages to loads of groups at once. This is known as spamming and is irritating because people have to pay to download several copies of the same message. So always look to see which groups another person has sent the message to (if any), before you reply and delete the ones that don't apply.

When replying to a message, edit out irrelevant parts of the previous post and type your reply under the relevant bits that are left. Your newsreader software should automatically add a line at the top of your message saying who posted the previous message when. Don't quote the whole of the previous message just to add "I agree" at the end of it. It tends to be annoying and doesn't add anything to the debate.

Both your e-mail software and your newsreader software should be able to add an automatic signature to your messages. Your signature shouldn't be more than four lines long (it's that supposed 'waste of Internet resources' business again). If you think you've got a good line in ASCII art, show it off in an ASCII art newsgroup, not in your signature.

DON'T SHOUT. IT'S HARD TO READ. Shouting is when you type in capital letters. The Net cops also say that you should always try to use correct English (if that is your chosen language, of course), and that you should use correct spelling and punctuation. On the other hand, they also say that you should never criticise someone for incorrect spelling or punctuation. This leaves them in something of a quandary because they get annoyed by bad spelling, but their own rules won't allow them do anything about it. Ha ha ha.

Oh, and one last piece of unnecessary advice – if you do happen to put a foot wrong and get an abusive reply to one of your posts, think carefully about what you want to say in return. Laws of libel and slander still apply on the Net as a couple of recent court cases have established, so don't rush off an abusive reply (also called a 'flame') too quickly.

Smileys

In the main, these are the devil's work. Little punctuation marks grouped together to make shorthand ways of expressing emotion, to wit, if you write a joke that isn't very funny, you can put a happy smiley :-) after it just to make sure everyone realises you're joking and doesn't take offence. For example:

> "Hugh was watching Divine do the lewd business and to his surprise she actually seemed to be enjoying herself. 'Blimey,' says Hugh, 'You're really enjoying that, aren't you?' 'No,' replies Divine, rather naughtily speaking with her mouth full, 'I'm just a much better actress than Liz.' :-)"

Other acceptable smileys include: :-(Sad or 'what a bummer' and… Er, that's it. There are tens, hundreds even of these foul little things, but ignore them all.

TLAs and ETLAs

Now these are nearly as bad as smileys, but not quite. Net cops will tell you that TLA stands for Three-Letter Acronym, and ETLA Extended Three-Letter Acronym (one with more than three letters) and they're right, except they're not. An acronym is a word formed from the initial letters of other words, such as radar or laser or RAM, but many of the TLAs and ETLAs that pop up on the Net are things like IMHO (In My Humble Opinion), ROTFL (Rolls On The Floor Laughing) and AFAIK (As Far As I Know). Unless you speak a very strange language, these are not pronounce-able as words, and so the 'A' should really stand for 'abbreviation', which would also encompass proper acronyms such as FOAD (Fuck Off And Die). Glad we've got that sorted then.

.net recommends

PC newsreaders

• Free Agent
ftp://ftp.dircon.co.uk/pub/tdc/internet/
windows/otherstuff/fagent10.zip
Probably the best PC newsreader in the world.

• Snews
ftp://ftp.demon.co.uk/pub/ibmpc/DIS/
snews129.zip
DOS-based newsreader for Windows haters.

Mac newsreaders

• Newswatcher
ftp://src.doc.ic.ac.uk/packages/mac-umich/util/
comm/usenet/newswatcher2.0b20.sit.hqx
The easiest program to set up and simple to use.

• Internews
ftp://src.doc.ic.ac.uk/packages/mac-umich/util/
comm/usenet/internews1.05.sit.hqx
Another good newsreader.

Take your pick from...

• Amiga
ftp://src.doc.ic.ac.uk/aminet/comm/uucp

• Archimedes
ftp://ftp.demon.co.uk/pub/archimedes/
developers

• Atari ST
ftp://src.doc.ic.ac.uk/packages/atari/umich/
Network/news

Chapter 7

Finding stuff

Gopher Menu

About the Electronic Frontier Foundation Gopher Server

About the Electronic Frontier Foundation

** ALERTS! - Action alerts on important and impending issues

** ELECTRONIC FRONTIER FOUNDATION FILES & INFORMATION

* Activism, Government & Freedom of Information

* Censorship/Free Expression/Intellectual Freedom

* Civil Liberties Misc.

* GII/NII/Open Platform/Information Infrastructure Policy

* Global and Non-U.S. Issues & Policy

* Graphics (EFF- and Net-related pics, WWW-server icons, etc.)

* Groups & Organizations Supporting the Online Community

* Intellectual Property/Patent/Trademark/Copyright

FTP and Gopher

The Net as an idea might well be lovely – all
those people using computers to bond in a
Nineties kinda way – but when it comes down to
it, much of the time online is spent with the aim
of getting your hands on as much free stuff as
possible.

Naturally, the desire to swap shareware programs and data became the impetus for the
development of two of the most important Net
tools of all – FTP and Gopher. FTP is what you
use to send files between two computers whilst
Gopher is sort of a method of indexing information on the Internet. Before the days of the World
Wide Web, Gopher was the golden boy in town,
blonde-haired, blue-eyed and immensely popular
because it made searching the Net for stuff a
doddle (well, by the rather clanking standards of
the time – and that was only four years ago).

These days, thanks to the rapid growth of the
Web, those two methods of storing and transfer-

ring files have lost popularity over the years. Having said that, you'll still find FTP and Gopher sitting hidden in the middle of your Web browsers – more on that in a minute.

FTP (which stands for File Transfer Protocol) is still a favoured way of transferring large files such as compressed programs (indeed, most Internet software is distributed by this method). The great advantage of the Net's something-for-nothing culture is that you can often FTP (download) the latest versions of Web browsers and newsreaders for free. Many of them are shareware, so if you intend to continue using them after the trial period you should check to see if a fee is payable.

Using FTP is much like listing files on a hard drive except, instead of searching through the files on your machine, you're trawling the disk of another computer on the Internet. Sometimes you need permission to access the files on a remote machine and sometimes you don't. If you don't, you're doing anonymous FTP. When the remote machine prompts you for a username you simply enter the word 'anonymous' and when you're prompted for your password it's good manners to tap in your e-mail address. Some sites check the password you've entered to make sure it looks like a valid e-mail address. With most Windows and Mac FTP software, you can set up the preferences so the software automatically passes an anonymous password and your e-mail address to the remote computer.

The whole enterprise sounds vaguely disreputable but it isn't. There's no real conspiracy beyond anonymous FTP other than in the Net's roots. Because of the Net's background in academia and the free flow of information, anonymous FTP was set up as a kind of way of leaving the door to your computer unlocked, so the neigh-

bours could get in and borrow a lawnmower or
something. Other FTP sites – those that aren't
anonymous – are more like leaving the door
locked and the key with just a few friends.

When you've connected to an FTP site, the
chances are you'll see a directory called pub,
which is short for 'public' and which is where all
the publicly accessible files will be kept. This
directory commonly has sub-directories which
describe the type of files in them, for example
graphics, Mac, PC or UNIX.

What happens next depends on the software
you're using. It's a good idea to download and
read any readme file in the root or pub directory.
This might give you information on when the
FTP site's maintainer would prefer you to access
it (usually not during local business or college
hours) and whether the site has any mirrors elsewhere on the Net. A mirror is an exact replica of
a site that's kept on a different machine – if
there's a mirror of a US site in the UK, downloads
will probably be quicker from the UK one.

Transferring files with FTP used to involve
typing in UNIX commands, but most Windows
and Mac FTP programs now enable you to do
the whole shebang with a point and a click
although you can still find UNIX ones if you're on
the look out for a laugh (erm, yes). It's definitely
worth getting hold of a point-and-click FTP program because it really does make things so
much easier.

Back to what we mentioned briefly earlier:
Many Web browsers, being the all-singing crea-
tures they are these days, now have FTP functions built in, so you just enter the address of an
FTP site in the Open Location box with ftp:// in
front of the address, instead of http://

Where do you want to go?

If you are wondering where you can go to access some FTP sites, keep reading. Perry Rover's major list of anonymous FTP sites is kept at the following FTP and Web locations:

http://140.111.1.22:8080/www.html

And there's an anonymous FTP FAQ at:

http://140.111.1.22:8080/www.html

You'll find that many files on FTP sites are compressed so they take up less disk space and less time to transfer over the Net (which in turn means lower phone bills). There are many different compression formats and to decompress the files to get them into a usable form you have to have the right compression program. Download David Lemson's Compression List from ftp://ftp.cso.uiuc.edu/doc/pcnet/compression for a run-down on what's what.

PC users can download compression utilities from ftp://garbo.uwasa.fi/pc/arcers while Mac users can check out a Web-based store at htpp://web.nexor.co.uk/mac-archive/

Some files come in a weird format called HQX which is a way of representing data like programs in ASCII text form. This may sound like a bizarre way of keeping important stuff in these days when everyone knows about bits and bytes, but a lot of the early Internet was text-only and this is a bit of a hangover from its pre-Imperial past.

If your FTP program gives you an error message saying that the FTP site was not accessible, it might be for several reasons. The most common one is that it's too busy and already has its quota of anonymous accesses. The reason for this is that every Internet computer, although designed for loads of people logging on to it at once, has its limits. And many Net computers are still based at universities, which will naturally give preference to access by their own students.

Another reason for an error message is that it's been taken temporarily off-line. In either of these cases try again later. If you can't access a site after several attempts at several different times, you can check whether it still exists by e-mailing a clever computer at service@nic.ddn.mil with the subject host [sitename] and no body message. It will eventually mail you back to tell you whether the site's still there or not.

And that, as they say, is FTP.

Tell me about this Gopher business

It had long been recognised by practised Net heads that the Net was a useful device but that actual interest in the thing wasn't going to keep growing unless there were better methods of finding one's way about it. After all, what use is a library without some means of finding the books you want? Programs like FTP were fine for transferring text and keep files together on a single computer, but as a method of indexing the files on loads of Net computers, it was useless.

Released (for free) in 1991, Gopher was a program designed to search the Internet. It came in two parts – to use Gopher, a person needed two things – a Gopher client and a Gopher server. A Gopher client is a program used by the user on his own home PC which allowed the user to type in the information he was looking for. This program would then send this information off to the Gopher server. The Gopher server is just another computer on the Net you connected to that had been set up to deal with Gopher searches.

The Gopher server contains large indexes which the Gopher client ruffles through on its searches. And there are many hundreds of Gopher servers all over the world, so if you are unable to find the information you're after on one server, you can usually jump to another and try it.

Actually using it, although not as easy as the Web, is not hard. It's a menu-based system, but it doesn't have the graphical splendour of the Web, though it is easier to use than FTP. Clicking through a Gopher menu is much like using Windows File Manager or the Mac's Finder. You're more likely to find academic reports and research papers on Gopher servers than you are on FTP sites, and less likely to find programs.

Gopher is clever because it's the remote Gopher server that does all the hard work – all your software has to do is send commands to the Gopher server. This means that you can access several Gopher sites at once, perform several Gopher searches at once and even download several files at once. To connect to a Gopher site all you have to do is type its name into your Gopher program by selecting 'new Gopher' or 'another Gopher' from the appropriate menu. Alternatively, you can prefix the name of the Gopher site with gopher:// in the Open Location box of your Web browser. The files listed on a Gopher menu do not actually have to be on that server, like using the Web, your Gopher program automatically connects you to the next server. All you have to do is go on pointing and clicking. Some good Gopher sites to get started with are:

wiretap.spies.com
heaps of cyberpunky information

gopher.eff.org
files from Net activists Electronic Frontier
Foundation

gopher.umn.edu
Project Gutenburg has electronic text from out-
of-copyright books

The results of a Gopher session, while a big
improvement over earlier search methods, still
tend to rely on the user knowing a bit of jargon.
And more often than not, Gopher rarely finds
what you were looking for straight away – several
goes are often needed, which usually return
loads of different inapplicable results anyway.
And if this does not work you have to try other
Gopher servers, which can be a bit inconvenient.
    An attempted solution to this was the intro-
duction of Veronica. Veronica was an extension
to Gopher developed at the University of Nevada
and it allowed the user to search not a single
Gopher server at a time, but all Gopher servers,
allowing you to narrow your search a bit while
you did it. Unfortunately, using Veronica was not
for the faint-hearted as it often involved the use
of nasty-looking control codes to do this. A typical search request might look something like
Joyce not Finnegan's Wake -t1, which translated
from nerdese, means "search all directories within Veronica for all references to the books of
James Joyce but do not include Finnegan's
Wake". Punchy but not the most user-friendly
system in the world.
    Another early search program was Archie
which existed to help the user find his way

around the various FTP sites on the Net. FTP, whilst excellent for transferring large files from an FTP site to your computer, is a dog if you don't know where the data you are after is kept. For instance, some FTP sites specialise in certain things – like Mac or PC software for instance, and if you didn't know the name of the site you were looking for, you could find yourself with problems.

Luckily, this is where Archie came in. Archie allowed the user to enter the name of the item they were looking for. Archie would then return the names of all the FTP sites that contained a reference to it.

To find a file with Archie, all you have to do is run your Archie program (obviously) type in a file name or part of a filename with a wildcard (for example news*.zip), and tell it to search the site archie.doc.ic.ac.uk which is a catalogue of what's on the Net's FTP site.

Alternatively, if you suspect that a file is on a specific FTP site, tap in the name of that site. Most Archie programs have built-in FTP routines so when all the sites that might have your file are listed, all you have to do is double-click on the file to download it.

Archie manages this in a similar manner to Gopher, in that a list of the contents (automatically updated) of about 1,000 FTP sites is held on various Archie servers.

Gopher, Archie and Veronica are still all in use now and are a must for people who use the Net as a serious information resource.

The Web, which in its latest incarnations has incorporated Gopher's functions, has more or less superseded these programs for the less serious user though. In fact, the writing was on the wall for Gopher even back in 1993 – throughout

1993, while Gopher usage grew at 997% per annum, the Web grew at 341,634% (according to Internet chronologer Robert H. Zakon).

Another largely superseded search device was WAIS, also invented in 1991. WAIS stands for Wide Area Information Servers and consists of a network of WAIS machines all containing databases of searchable information.

Generally, WAIS is used to search for text documents but has fallen out of favour because using it requires more specialised knowledge than Gopher.

For instance, a couple of years ago, to use WAIS, a user would have to telnet to a WAIS server – and telnet, although a useful program, is not the kind of thing to muck about with unless there's a good reason and your mum knows about it beforehand.

Once you'd gone through this barbaric procedure and had arrived at your destination, you'd find that many WAIS servers relied on UNIX-style combinations of commands and that's not for the novice user either.

But you can still use it. Using WAIS is similar to wading through a catalogue. Entries on a WAIS server are organised in alphabetical order – into categories like aeronautics, agriculture and so on and searches can be made on those categories.

More modern versions of WAIS have been developed to cope with video and sound files and there are now easier-to-use graphical systems available which contain all the telnetting bits and bobs in an more accessible package.

But again, the growth of the Web has left even these innovations looking a bit long in the tooth.

We recommend...

FTP software

Windows
• WS_FTP
ftp://ftp.usma.edu/pub/msdos/winsock.files/
Deliciously friendly point-and-click Scottie dog
affair.

Mac
• Anarchie
ftp://mac.archive.umich.edu/man/util/comm
A combined Archie and FTP program.

Gopher software

Windows
• WS Gopher
ftp://dewey.tis.inel.gov/pub/wsgopher/
Gobbles memory, slightly dicky, but still great.

Mac
• Turbogopher
ftp://mac.archive.umich.edu/mac/util/comm/
gopher/
Not bad and familiar to Mac users in its look and
feel.

Chapter 8

The World Wide Web

The World Wide Web is one of the main reasons for the massive increase in the Net's popularity among the not-so-computer literate. The Web was developed at the European Laboratory for Particle Physics in Switzerland (which is also known as CERN) in 1990, and during the early part of 1995 it became the most popular means of accessing information on the Internet, largely because it is so much easier to navigate than other, older parts of the Net.

Its point-and-click hypertext control system makes cruising the Internet a breeze because the Web enables you to do almost everything with the mouse. No typing of long commands, no logging in and out of computers, no keeping track of what you were doing. The only exception is when you have to type in the address of a new page to visit in your Web browser – the program you use to access the Web. And even this can be automated (or 'bookmarked') if it is a page you return to frequently. Through using the Web, text, graphics, sound and video can be sent over the Internet, making it by far the sexiest part of the Net, and many of the hottest new software developments are for Web-based applications.

The World Wide Web gives you a graphical interface with which to navigate the Internet. Text and pictures become hypertext links (see the section on HTML for more on what this means) which you can click on to access other Web pages, whether they're on the same computer as the first or an entirely different machine. The program you need to access the World Wide Web is called a Web browser, and these are available for all the popular computer formats – PC and Mac users are particularly spoilt for choice. Issue Ten of .net magazine has a comprehensive round-up of currently available Web browsers, and several are featured later in this chapter.

When you run a Web browser, it automatically connects to a home page – the default for Netscape Navigator is Netscape Communications' home page. You can scroll this page up and down to read the text, and you can use the hypertext links to jump to another page. Any text that is highlighted in blue is a hypertext link, and clicking on it will tell the browser to download another page of information. It doesn't matter where the new page is stored, the Web browser connects to it automatically.

All World Wide Web pages are created using HyperText Markup Language (HTML) which started as a simple way of formatting text and has now expanded to include commands for integrating pictures, video, sound and even forms which you can fill in on-line. HTML is a standard language that everyone on the Web has implemented, but the rapid commercialisation of the Web has meant that companies rather than academic organisation have more of a stake in its future. Net purists are worried that companies such as Netscape, which has added its own extensions to HTML, are trying to distort the development of the Net in their favour. The purists argue that the whole success of the Net is based on commonly agreed and implemented open standards, and that proprietary developments are not only an anathema to the way the Net works, but threaten its continued success. On the other hand, it could be argued that vigorous companies are far more likely to get things done than committees of beards who sit around umming and ahhing for months.

The Web in action

Actually being on the Web operates slightly differently to being on other parts of the Internet. The first thing to notes is that you only ever connect to the computer at the other end (the 'Web server') whenever you click on a hyperlink. This explains why sometimes when you are already at a Web page, clicking on another page contained at that site sometimes means you get told that the server is busy, and access is denied. It's for this slightly annoying reason that Netscape have built in that handy 'Stop' icon.

Secondly, it's important to realise that although other parts of the Net update themselves happily (because someone actually looks after them – for instance, WAIS or Gopher servers), this does not apply to the Web. Unfortunately, this is the downside of the hypertext system – there's no way to know for sure whether the site you are attempting to link to even exists any more. In this case, it's really up to the Web page owner to make sure that any links contained in his or her page are still active. This is especially annoying if you have lots of bookmarked sites – thankfully, the newer Web browsers allow you to edit your bookmark lists and get rid of the ones that are no longer active.

Just like with other parts of the Net, it's sometimes impossible to access a Web page because it's just very popular (often the case with many

American sites). In this case, you just have to keep trying (the best way is to wait until it's night-time in America, and then try – when all your competitors will be in bed). The alternative is to wait until the site owners upgrade their equipment to handle more accesses.

Finally, those who are real experts will try to look for a Web page's mirror site. This is nothing more than a duplicate site kept elsewhere, so if everyone is accessing location A, all you have to do is nip along to its mirror kept at location B – if there is one. Some of the big sites – like the Cardiff Movie Database- have mirror sites in America, Europe and the Far East. The general rule of thumb is to only access sites in your geo-graphical area (however, you can always cheat by nipping along to further afield, although it's not encouraged because it puts additional strain on the Net).

Netscape itself is one company with a multi-tude of mirror sites, hardly a surprise when you consider the number of people using the compa-ny's products and the necessity to nip along to its Web site every now and again to see what's new. If you find you can't connect to it via the built-in 'home' function in every Netscape brows-er, you can try:

ftp://wuarchive.wust1.edu/packages/www/Netscape/

ftp://ftp.cps.cmich.edu/pub/netscape/

ftp://server.berkeley.edu/pub/netscape/

ftp://sunsite.doc.ic.ac.uk/computing/information-systems/www/Netscapes/

ftp://ftp.luth.se/pub/infosystems/www/netscape/
netscape/

(Note that all these contain the latest shareware
version of the Netscape browser and do not supply technical support – for that, you'll have to
keep plugging away at the Netscape's own home
pages.)

Getting going

Assuming you have your Web browser set-up
correctly (something your service provider will
help you with if they're any good), to get going,
all you have to do is type in the address of the
Web page you wish to visit at the space near the
menu bar, which should have something like
URL: printed next to it.

Where do you find Web page addresses
from? These days, just about everywhere. Plenty
of adverts have them attached, and magazines
like .net and .net Directory publish huge lists of
interesting sites to visit each month. You can
always tell a Web address from another Internet
address because it always starts with 'http://'.
Other internet addresses, like FTP sites, start with
'ftp://'.

What's with this URL term though? It's another acronym unfortunately but it isn't necessary to
think about it too much. All it means is 'Uniform
Resource Locator' and hopefully that's all you'll
ever need to know about it.

But anyway, back to the here and now. World
Wide Web addresses (anything starting in http://)
look very complicated but are really quite easy to
understand. They are made up of several distinct
parts. Let's take .net's home page address as an
example:

http://www.futurenet.co.uk/netmag/net.html

http:// tells the Web browser that it is making a World Wide Web connection. New Web browsers such as Enhanced Mosaic and Netscape Navigator enable you to access other Net resources such as FTP and Gopher sites. To access these, the URL would start ftp:// or gopher://. You can work out what you'd type to access a Telnet site.

www.futurenet.co.uk/ is the location of the Web server, the computer that the pages are stored on.

netmag/net.html is the directory path and the filename of Web page; the directory is netmag/ and the filename is net.html

    To enter a Web address you want to connect to, use the Open Location command from the File menu – some browsers may have a slightly different command such as Open URL – and type the URL of the page you want to connect to in the box. Click on the OK button and wait for the browser to connect.

Accessing newsgroups with a Web browser

If your service provider has a news server, you can access the newsgroups through a Web browser rather than running a separate news-reader program (although this can often be a little slow, depending on your service provider's set-up). In the preferences option of your Web browser there will be an option for you to enter the name of the news server you wish to connect to (it might be called NNTP Server). If you have an account with a service provider, they'll provide you with the name of the news server. If you have a university account, or an account through your office network, you'll have to get the name of the news server from the system administrator. The news server name is normally the domain name of the service provider with the word news in front.

You can send e-mail from a Web page by clicking on a hypertext e-mail address which activates the browser's built-in e-mail function. To enable your Web browser to send e-mail, you enter the name of your mailserver and your e-mail address into the preferences option, for example nmerritt@futurenet.co.uk as the e-mail address and mailhost.futurenet.co.uk as the mailserver address. Again, check with your service provider or system administrator for your own specific details.

When you want to access a specific newsgroup, say uk.media for pointless discussions about media in the UK, you'd enter news:uk. media in the Open Location box (when you've set up all your preferences and that, of course).

Accessing FTP and Gopher with a browser

As mentioned previously, most of the newer browsers have FTP built-in. To get it going, it should be no more difficult that typing the address of the FTP site at the space reserved for typing in URLs (prefixed by 'ftp://' instead of 'http://'). Likewise for Gopher sites.

But my computer can't display pictures!

It's a tragic state of affairs, but some companies and universities with prehistoric gear are unable to take full advantage of the Web. However there is an imperfect solution. Not too long ago, the entire Web was text-only and special text-only browsers were developed to deal with this. The answer in this case is something called Lynx. If you are trying to access the Web from a site with text-only facilities, ask your systems manager if he has Lynx . If so, when you get it working, you won't be able to see pictures but you will be able to read text and follow any hyperlinks to other Web pages. However, there is one problem. Lynx was designed to work with older versions of HTML – and some of the newer de-facto standards from the likes of Netscape might not be compatible. Unfortunately, there's only one real way to figure out how this is going to affect you, and that's by giving it a go and seeing what happens.

Run that jargon by me again

Home page
: The welcome or index page on a Web site is known as the home page. The home page for .net is http://www.futurenet.co.uk/netmag/net.html/

HTML
: HyperText Markup Language, a simple computer language for creating World Wide Web pages (see separate chapter on HTML).

http://
: HyperText Transfer Protocol, the transmission protocol used for sending World Wide Web data over the Internet. When you type in the address of a Web page you want to connect to,

	entering http:// tells your Web browser to use the correct protocol.
https://	HyperText Transfer Protocol Secure, new version of http with data encryption built-in enabling sensitive financial information to be transmitted over the World Wide Web. Netscape Navigator and the new commercial Netsite server software already have encryption built-in as standard.
Link	Area of text, image or icon on a Web page that connects you to another Web page or file. Also known as a hyperlink or even as a hypertext link.
Lynx	A Web browser for computer systems that can only display text.
URL	Uniform Resource Locator, the address of a Web page.
Mirror site	A 'spare' copy of the Web pages kept at another location, to reduce the load on the main site.

Software ahoy!

There's no need to pay through the nose for a commercial Web browser as part of an expensive package – you can get a Web browser for your computer from the Internet. While most browsers are freeware, Netscape and NCSA Mosaic are shareware – you're supposed to pay around $29 for a single-user version of Netscape, for example.

Every Web browser you download has a license agreement of some sort attached to it. Read this document before you use the browser. As with any other shareware, you should pay for any applications used on a regular basis.

.net recommends

PC Windows

• NCSA Enhanced Mosaic for Windows
ftp:// ftp.ncsa.uiuc.edu/Mosaic/Windows
Old, slightly tarnished gold, but the latest version of Enhanced Mosaic is looking good.

• Netscape Navigator
ftp://ftp.mcom.com/netscape/windows/ and download the latest version.
The best browser you'll find anywhere.

• WinWeb for Windows
ftp://ftp.einet.net/einet/pc/winweb/winweb.zip
Fast, but not exactly overflowing with features.

Apple Mac

• MacWeb
ftp://ftp.einet.net/einet/mac/macweb/macweb.
latest.sea.hqx
Simple and easy to use. Lacking in features.

• Netscape Navigator
ftp://ftp.mcom.com/netscape/mac/
It's the best on the PC and it's the best on the Mac too.

Amiga

• Mosaic for the Amiga
ftp://ftp.demon.co.uk/pub/amiga/mosaic/
Mosaic_1.2_AmiTCP/lha
As good a browser as you'll find for Escom's
adopted son.

Acorn Archimedes

• ArcWeb
ftp://ftp.demon.co.uk/www/arcweb_0.19.arc
A good browser, and there's not much to choose
between it and...

• Webster
ftp://ftp.demon.co.uk/developers/webster006.arc
Which also happens to be a rather rinky dink
kind of program.

Atari ST

• Lynx
ftp://src.doc.ic.ac.uk/computing/systems/atari/
umich/Mint/Network/
A text-only browser, but it's all ST and Falcon
users have got.

UNIX

• Netscape Navigator
ftp://ftp.mcom.com/netscape/unix/
Look, it's the best there is, OK?

Chapter 9

HTML

```
                          FutureNet
<HTML>
<HEAD>
<TITLE>FutureNet</TITLE>
</HEAD>
<BODY bgcolor="#FFFFFF">
<CENTER>
<P>
<FONT SIZE=+2><B>Europe's most popular e-zine - updated daily</B></FONT><BR>
<IMG SRC="http://www.futurenet.co.uk/Images/Logos/Futurenetlogo.gif" WIDTH=328
HEIGHT=150></CENTER><P>
<UL>
<FONT SIZE=+2><B><LI>World news</B></FONT> -

All the top news stories, updated every weekday<BR>
<FONT SIZE=+2><B><LI>Computing</B></FONT> -

Hundreds of features on PC, Mac, ST, Amiga and more<BR>


<FONT SIZE=+2><B><LI>Videogames</B></FONT> -

Loads of game reviews and features for every platform<BR>
```

Damn, it's another Net acronym. Unfortunately for acronym haters, it's also hugely important, describing as it does the glue that holds the World Wide Web together and therefore the whole current interest in the Internet. HTML is what makes the Netscape browser work, prints Web pages on-screen and links one Web page with another. Without HTML, there could be no Internet as it currently exists.

There are two approaches to dealing with HTML – you can cheerfully ignore it, filing it away as another one of those Net acronyms you need to remember, but will rarely use. Or you can learn a little more about it and understand some of the detail about how the World Wide Web operates. Thankfully, it helps that as computery languages go, HTML is so simple as to make a nun curse with joy.

So HTML is a computer language, but it's not like other computer languages such as BASIC. It doesn't so much as tell a computer what to do, as tell a hypertext document (more on that in a minute) what to contain. For the moment, it's enough to know that it is HTML that tells the Web browser what and how to print the text and pictures on a Web page. (If you are familiar with PostScript and what it does, it's not too far off the same kind of idea, although miles simpler.)

A typical HTML document contains text that someone might want to appear on a Web page, plus instructions on how to display that text – on a white background, in red letters two inches high, for example. It also contains information about where the Web browser can find a picture for the Web page (and where to put it) and most importantly of all, HTML contains a link to another Web page. This link is usually what you see as a blue underlined bit of text on a Web page, and in the trade, it is known as a hyperlink. It is this facility which allows the Web to exist at all.

What is hypertext?

This ability to link text documents together reached its heights at Apple Computer, the first company to exploit this technology in a ground-breaking program called HyperCard. Its great advantage was its massive flexibility in linking different kinds of information together.

A series of related hypertext documents is called a Hypertext stack, and in effect, the entire World Wide Web is nothing more than a related series of hypertext documents joined into a gigantic Hypertext stack.

However, it is the Web and HTML that has been the garden in which hypertext has flowered. The reason for this takes us back to the original inventors of the Web, those wild and groovy guys (ahem) at the CERN particle physics research facility. These days, particle physics is a massive multinational affair with researchers scattered all over Europe and CERN is the biggest such undertaking in the world.

Creating a database system which allowed the scientists to communicate their findings to each other over the Net was not an easy thing to do whilst retaining flexibility, but the task was cracked by Tim Berners-Lee in 1990. But whilst CERN began building the Web, something else was needed to spark the interest of the rest of the world.

That spark arrived in 1993 when the US National Centre for Supercomputing Applications released their Mosaic browser into the Public Domain. At a stroke, the general Internet user could get onto the Web using a simple point-and-click interface. Perhaps more than any other recent innovation, it was the release of Mosaic that put the Internet on the map.

As for HTML itself, it used to be largely under the control of the standards set by the Internet Society, who are largely responsible for specifying the technical basis of the Net. But in these increasingly commercial times, control of HTML has really passed to the commercial sector in the shape of Netscape, makers of the Net's most widely-used browsers. Their market power allows them to dictate standards much to the chagrin of their rivals, but in the main this has worked fine for the user as most Web page designers have been happy to follow their lead.

Creating your own Web pages

We're not going to try to provide an in-depth tutorial here as plenty of good ones already exist.

But just for the sake of completeness, we'll go into a few of the ideas just to show you how easy it is if you do decide you'd like to have a go.

The first thing you have to do is distinguish between HTML instructions and the documents the instructions create. The easiest way to do this is to take a look at any Web page. If you call up a Web page from within Netscape (assuming this is the browser you are using), what you are seeing – all the nice graphics and formatted text – is the document created by HTML. To get a look at the actual HTML instructions, all you have to do is go to the 'View' menu item within Netscape, and select 'Source'. The document displayed changes and you'll see loads of text but surrounded by symbols that look like this: <h1> or <A HREF="http://www.futurenet.co.uk/magazines/pc _format.html">. These are the actual HTML commands and mean stuff like 'make the text following the command <h1> header text' or 'if someone clicks on this bit of blue text, load in the Web page for PC Format magazine'.

Happily, the requirement to know any HTML at all these days to create your own Web pages is rapidly vanishing as new graphically-based Web page editing packages become available. Designers familiar with QuarkXpress will soon have access to a plug-in which will allow them to create HTML documents from within Quark itself and there are already stand-alone packages available from Netscape themselves – nip along to http://www.netscape.com/ to check them out.

Chapter 10

Java

After all the hype about Netscape, e-mail and all the rest of it, it's hard to remember sometimes that the Internet is a rapidly-evolving entity. No sooner has one flash in the pan faded away that there's another one not too far off detonation.

If the big sensation over the last couple of years has been the World Wide Web and, in particular, Netscape, the next one might well be Java, from makers of powerful scientific workstations Sun MicroSystems. It's not just being heralded as a funky new piece of software but as the tool which could destroy the PC, Microsoft and Intel, and herald a new type of machine – the NC or Net Computer. But what is it? Why all the excitement? And have people perhaps gotten a little too carried away already?

What is it all about?

Up until the Mosaic Web browser was invented a couple of years ago, the trend in Internet software had been for people to use small stand-alone programs to do small, specific things, like send e-mail or exchange opinions over Usenet. So there was a bewildering array of stuff to choose from – FTP programs, e-mail programs, newsreaders and all the rest of it. People liked it like that and it was just the way it was going to be, and no more of these new-fangled ideas please, I've been on the Net for decades and no mistake.

Until the first Web browsers started to appear, that is. Slowly, other programs began, heretically, to get integrated into these programs until the situation today where Netscape 2.0 can do everything except walk the dog and stick Grandma back in her nursing home at 6pm on Sunday.

This approach has been the bedrock of software development for years – witness the fact the wordprocessor used to write this book would have taken up no more than 500K of memory five or so years ago, yet Microsoft World 6 requires something like 60Mb of disk space now, largely because features have been added which few people use but they pay for anyway. It meant software companies could release upgrades and charge the consumer loads of money for the privilege and it is one of the reasons why the likes of Microsoft have become so powerful.

The Internet allows a different approach though and it's one tightly bound-up with a very old mixed in with a brand-new way of thinking about computers. It's a little complicated but here goes:

Instead of the current situation, where we have extremely powerful, expensive desktop computers all networked together (and largely wasting all that power on menial tasks), an alternative approach is to get rid of the extras and develop cheaper computers focused on specific tasks, connect them to much more powerful computers on the Internet and then allow them to download automatically only the software they need to perform their tasks. The computers (called NCs or Network Computers) are currently being developed by companies like Sun Microsystems and Apple but the software needed to make these computers work properly is already here – Java.

What is Java?

Java is basically a programming language that has been integrated with the World Wide Web. It allows Web pages to contain little bits of programming code which, for the first time, allow the page to do more than simply display text and graphics. So a Web page can now contain little rolling demos, sound, scrolling adverts – whatever you like. The clever part though is that in a nod to this idea of network computing, none of the Java code is actually contained in the Web page itself – instead, it is downloaded automatically when it is needed. But the impetus for this is not just to jazz up Web pages with funky extras, it's to develop new types of programs which can exploit the power of the Web to the full. Like company spreadsheets which automatically get updated with new information on raw materials prices or the latest stock prices, for instance. Or even new versions of software which update themselves over the Net, automatically, getting rid of the need to visit your computer store for the latest features.

So it's no surprise that the likes of Microsoft have announced that they'll be including Java support in Windows 95, that Barclays Bank are attending Java conferences – and that Java has been hailed by some as a breakthrough development which could turn the computing industry on its head.

The little bits of Java code, downloaded when needed, are called applets and, in perhaps the

cleverest move of all, will work on any computer.
It doesn't matter whether you look at a Web
page incorporating applets on a PC or a
Macintosh – Java will know and will make sure it
will work.

Java has been behind much of the recent
interest in 3D-based Web front-ends. Ideally,
companies working in this area would like to be
able to create full 3D virtual world-type interfaces
but the reality of slow Net connections places
severe constraints on how fast this type of technology will be able to develop.

Although Java is up and running now, its current incarnation as a Web curiosity is only the
first step in possible clash between PCs and the
coming NCs. If you remember that Java applets
are only downloaded to the computer when they
are needed, it's not hard to see how NCs – which
rely on the same concept to keep costs down –
will work with it.

This approach will allow manufacturers to
develop new types of computer – handheld Web
browser/mobile phones, TV set-top multimedia
systems using on-line services to download the
latest software – and sitting at the heart of it all
will be a program you can have a play with now
if you want. To do so, nip along to
http://java.sun.com/ and have a go.

Java in action

Assuming you've nipped along to the Java site,
you'll want to see some stuff in action. To this
end, Sun, understandably proud of their new
baby, have already developed what they claim is
the first Java-based NC. Called the JavaStation, it
debuted to not very much enthusiasm at all in
the UK although Sun are pointing out that they

want to pitch it at internal company networks first. The idea is that a user would use, say, a basic text editor and download applets for formatting text, bolding text or whatever when needed. It's hard at the moment to see how this offers much of an advantage over the current way of doing things (assuming the file server all these JavaStations would be hooked into could stand the strain). And it's certainly impossible to imagine the Net, slow enough as it is at the moment, being able to handle home-based JavaStations quickly. As for the security implications – one of the strongest laws of data security is: never let a program download anything without warning the user first. Java as it is currently set up could be a recipe for virus attacks, hackers and goodness knows whatever else to gain access to your most sensitive information.

But even if NCs aren't yet ready to carry the flag into battle against the PC, Java may well have a bright future as part of the World Wide Web. Although there are no software programs available which can use Java, apart from Netscape, nip along to http://www.sun.com/ to see Java in action.

What's in it for me?

Well, in all honesty, absolutely nothing at the moment, unless you fancy yourself as a hotshot Web page designer and you want to stay abreast of current developments. It's not clear yet whether Java is anything more than a gimmick or really is the next HTML – i.e. a tool that could define how the Net evolves over the next five years. And until people can think of ways to make Java really do something useful on the Web, it's unlikely this situation will change. But it's quite a neat idea as ideas go and there are going to be some neat-looking Web pages around before long. The true test will be how the Net community responds to it and starts taking it in directions Java's designers didn't think of. Hopefully, that day is not going to be too far off.

Jargon killed

Argh! What does all this jargon mean?

NC	a network computer. A cut-down PC, it's had all the expensive bits taken out meaning costs can be reduced. Instead, everything it needs it takes from a network as and when required.
Java	a new network-based programming language which is clever in two ways: (1) It only sends the bits of itself a computer needs to use at any one time and (2) it works on any computer, meaning computer users don't have to think about the type of software they are downloading any more.
Applet	a little program for a very specific purpose, written in Java.
HotJava	Sun's own Java-compatible Web browser.

Chapter 11

Internet Relay Chat

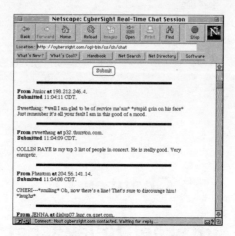

You could be missing out on one of the Net's most entertaining areas if your view of the Net is restricted to newsgroups and the World Wide Web. Internet Relay Chat (IRC) is a real-time chat system where what you type appears as you type it on the screens of all those tuned into the same channel as you. IRC isn't sexy, it doesn't have groovy pictures and sound samples plastered all over it, but for sheer entertainment value it's hard to beat.

IRC started out in Finland, where its creator Jarkko Oikarinen decided in 1988 to improve on the simple UNIX 'talk' program. The 'talk' command establishes a text link between your computer and that of your conversation partner. IRC took the principle several steps further, enabling computers to talk over lots of different chat lines, with tens or even hundreds of people gossiping away on each one. You can even be in more than one room at a time, having two sets of conversations with two different groups of people.

IRC is not a network of machines, it is a pro-

tocol for communication between machines, just
the same way that FTP, or HTTP, or Telnet, or
Gopher are. There are two main IRC networks –
EFNet and the Undernet. EFNet is the larger of
the two networks, and when people talk about
IRC, they generally mean EFNet.

And it works like this...

IRC is a classic client-server system. The servers
are the machines on the Net that transmit all the
chatting around the world, much like television
transmitters that broadcast hopeless sitcoms and
gritty dramas. There are servers located at various
strategic locations around the globe. The clients
are the TV aerials on people's houses that pick up
the programmes, or rather the chat. A client is
the program that runs on your machine and
interprets all the data that the IRC server sends to
your computer and makes it all as understand-
able as possible. Some clients are better than
others – Windows people have it easy, UNIX
users don't – you can find out where to get an
IRC client for your computer at the end of this
chapter.

Once your client is installed, you need to find
an IRC server to connect to (as always, there's a
list later in the chapter – you know the drill).
Once you've started the IRC client, if you haven't
been automatically connected to a server, or if
you have and the server you're on is in the middle of nowhere, you can change server by either
issuing the /server <new server name> command
if you're using a text client, or selecting the command from the menu in a graphical client.

When you connect to a server, you'll get a
welcome screen telling you a bit about the server
and then you're on your own in IRCland, with

only a few thousand complete strangers waiting to talk to you. The next thing to do is join a channel. A channel in IRC is like a room in a house where people will be chatting away. Just about every channel on IRC is identified by a hash (#) before the name of the channel, for example #poker. Two good general channels to pile into are #england and #ircbar. #england has lots of English people on it. #ircbar is a cool place to hang out – there's even a barman there who will make you a (virtual) drink.

To join a channel, you just type the command /join <channel name> (all commands in IRC begin with a forward slash, unless you're using a fancy Window client). Once in a channel, you'll be given a list of the people on that channel. Some people will have @ signs next to their name which signifies that they are channel operators who run the channel. They can kick people out and even bar people for good so be nice.

So, you've joined a channel. If it's your first time on a talker of any description, be warned – you may not be able to assimilate all the information that comes across. You will see a lot of words that you don't understand. This is because people can't generally type as fast as they think, and as such tend to abbreviate words, but stick with it, and get talking to people. The people on IRC are a usually friendly bunch, and most of them can remember the fact that they were once newcomers and will be only to happy to help you out.

Bored of that already?

As it stands, there are two networks of IRC servers – EFNet and the Undernet. EFNet is by far the bigger of the two networks, comprising lots of servers, whereas the Undernet has only a handful. Some people don't like EFNet, they say it's too big and too politicised. They also point out that there are many 'Net splits' on EFNet, which is when two servers stop talking to each other and create two separate IRC sessions, which gets annoying because it's like having a group conversation split into two. Similarly, these people are peeved that a lot of the server operators don't know what they're doing.

These people didn't just sit around and whinge, though. They created the Undernet, which is a smaller IRC network, but with more helpful server operators and a smaller crowd of users (around ten per cent of the number on EFNet). It's supposed to be a lot friendlier, but you'd be hard pushed to tell the difference between EFNet and the Undernet. To connect to the Undernet is simple – you just change server with the /server command. The Undernet people have made it very simple to connect to a server – there are many servers, but only three addresses altogether (see later). You'll find that many of your favourite EFNet channels are replicated on the Undernet, and all the commands are the same – you're still using IRC, just on different servers.

Service with a smile

A list of servers follows for your chatting pleasure.

EFNet servers

• supercomputer.swan.ac.uk 6667
Swansea University. Only accepts .ac.uk domains, so it's one for the students.

• serv.eng.abdn.ac.uk 6667
Often very busy.

• stork.doc.ic.ac.uk 6667
Takes connections from commercial sites.

• dismayl.demon.co.uk 6667
Demon Internet's IRC server.

• cismhp.univ-lyon1.fr 6667
French but pretty quick and it accepts hits from
all UK sites.

• irc.funet.fi 6667
Fast and in Finland.

Undernet servers

• uk.undernet.org 6667
For the UK.

• us.undernet.org 6667
For the US.

• eu.undernet.org 6667
For Europe.

I command you to obey

These are the most common IRC commands.
There are some which can screw up your
account, so if someone tells you to type a string
of commands you don't recognise, don't do it.
Hackers like to prey on newbies and con them
into typing dodgy commands. All IRC commands
are preceded by a forward slash /. In this list, any
compulsory parameters will be enclosed in pointy
brackets <>. Optional modifiers are in braces.

/join <channel name>
The simplest of them all. Enables you to join a
channel. If the value of NOVICE is set to ON, you
will automatically leave the current channel.

/leave <channel name>
Amazingly enough, this lets you leave a channel.

/list max <n>min <n>t
Will list all the IRC channels. You can use wildcards (for example /list *sex) will list all the channels with the word sex in them. The -max and -
min modifiers enable you to list less than or the
same number of users than the value of -max.
So, /list -min and max 3 *sex will list all the channels with sex in their names AND with either two
or three users on them. Finally, -t will only list
channels with topics set. The topic is the little
body of text next to the channel's name.

/mag <username> <message>
Will sent a private message to <user name> and
that person only, the content of which is in
<message>. Can be shortened to /ms on IRC 2
clients. To send a message to the last person who
sent you a message, use a comma instead of
their name. So, say Mr Longname just sent me a
message. Rather than type his whole name
again, I just type /mag, Go away silly bloke!

/me <action>
This enables you to do actions. For example, if I
typed /me laughs, on the output Window everyone would see 'nmerritt laughs'.

/whois
This is one you'll use quite a lot. /whois gives you
all the info that IRC has on a user – their e-mail

address, their server name, the domain they're
connecting from, the channels they're connecting from and the channels they're on. Use this
before you go to a private channel with a sup-
posedly female user, just to make sure you're not
having Net sex with Bill Clinton.

/who Name
Just typing /who will list all the users currently
logged in, the channel they're on and their e-
mail address. A cut-price version of /whois.
However you can also specify a channel name,
and therefore find out who is on a certain
channel. You can also specify wildcards for
domain names.

/set novice off
The /set command is pretty big and covers a few
things, but this part of the command is the one
you'll use the most. When you initially log on to
IRC, unless you're using a custom client, you'll
only be allowed on one channel at a time –
when you join another channel, the client automatically /leaves you from the other channel. By
setting the value of NOVICE to OFF, you can be
on more than one channel at the same time.

/nick <new nickname>
Enables you to change your username. It's good
if you're using a bog standard client, because
they take your UNIX user id as your nickname,
and it's no fun wandering around IRC with a dull
nickname like rlonghurst.

Come chat with me

Channels change all the time so there's no guar-
antee that any of these will be there when you

look them up, but these are some of .net's more permanent favourites.

#poker	On-line poker. Whatever next?
#england	English people hang out here
#ircbar	Meet and chat to strangers
#eliza	A pretend friend just for you
#reddwarf	Sci-fi TV chat
#vampire	Bloodsuckers galore
#startrek	Gnnnnnngggghh
#beastsex	Don't worry, it's not a real sheep

Chatting software here

You can get hold of an IRC client from the Northern Europe Sunsite at Imperial College. The main address is ftp://src.doc.ic.ac.uk/ computing/comms/irc/clients and then /pc/ or /macintosh/ or /elisp/ if you're one of those people who likes EMACS, or even /vms/ if you have a VAX handy.

If you're using a UNIX box, the relevant client software is in the irc/clients directory.

The finest IRC client on the whole world is WSIRC for Windows. If you're into IRC, it's a great excuse to buy a PC. It takes an ugly text-based front end and turns it into a beautiful graphical interface, with buttons to do absolutely anything. So, got a PC? Get WSIRC.

As far as the Mac goes, you have a choice of either Homer or Ircle. And UNIX? Well, you're stuck with good old IRCII, the ancestor of them all.

Amiga owners should keep an eye out for Grapevine which is available from ftp://ftp. demon.co.uk/pub/amitcp/extras/ grapevine-1_33.lha

What about the Web?

IRC seems a little old-fashioned in these Web-powered days, so it's hardly a surprise to hear that there's a Web IRC facility now. The advantage here is that all you need is a copy of Netscape – so no IRC messing about here. For a pretty good list of WebChat pages, it's best to check Yahoo (http://www.yahoo.com/Computers_and_Internet/Internet/World_Wide_Web/Communication) or Axl's Ultimate Home Page (http://www.osha.igs.net/~axe/chatsite.html) which has over 120 links. Or you can try these...

1. Cybersight Real-Time Chat Session
http://cybersight.com/cgi-bin/cs/ch/chat
One of the first, still one of the best.

2. Tribal Voice – The Pow Wow Page
http://tribal.com/powwow/
Best if you are new to the chat business.

3. Star Wars Chat
http://www.irsociety.com/cgi-bin/webchat_door-way.cgi?Room=Star_Wars
Talk about Those Films.

4. SportsChat
http://www.4-lane.com/sportschat/
Talk about that stuff involving exercise, like.

Chapter 12

Telnet

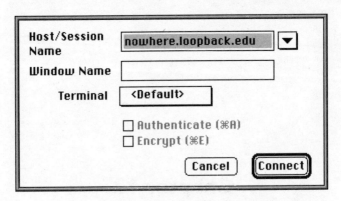

You can do some really sneaky things with the
Internet. You can sit at a computer screen in
one country and take control of a machine on
the other side of the world. The commands you
type in on a screen in, say, Birmingham, will be
executed on a machine in Boston and the computer in Boston knows to send the results to
your screen.

This magical process is called Telnet, and
even though it's possibly the most archaic way to
connect to another computer on the Internet, it
has many practical applications. When
RainbowNet was running a cybercafe at
Glastonbury, US students kept on coming in to
Telnet to their university computers so they could
check their e-mail accounts (and no doubt also
to brag about what a 'cooool' time they were
having at Glasters).

Telnet is entirely text-based, and gives you
the same kind of interface that you'd use to log
on to a standard BBS service. You can only Telnet
to systems that offer public access, or those on
which you have a private account. In the UK,
there are also Telnet sites which enable you to
use other Internet tools like Gopher and Archie.

Computer-literate students often use Telnet to access remote news servers when their university's server refuses to take the alt.binaries.pictures.erotica newsgroups.

Once you've connected to the host computer and logged on, most Telnet sites employ generic passwords, so you can use the system as if you're directly connected to it. In other words, you use the remote system to access and retrieve files in much the same way you'd access data on your PC, rooting around for interesting documents and messages. This means you can open accounts on BBSs and on-line services all over the world. Instead of calling them direct using your modem, you just connect to your local PoP and Telnet directly in. And you don't necessarily have to Telnet a system on the other side of the planet either. Many BBSs in the UK are accessible using Telnet, so you can always connect to them by making a local call instead of a costly long-distance phone call.

There are many different kinds of Telnet site. Some are just like BBSs, with lively message bases; others are like vast reference libraries with all kinds of ancient and modern material available for downloading. Take a look at some of the sites listed below and see what takes your fancy. Many Telnet servers only enable you to access certain parts of the system by entering the appropriate port number into the URL. If the port number is 70, you just enter it into the Port box in the Connect window of your Telnet client software. Port 23 is normally the default.

Telnet servers run on many different types of computer systems, and even the same types of systems may use different software. This means you may have to learn different commands depending on the system you're connected to.

It's not all bad, though, because almost all Telnet
sites use menu-based command systems. The
problems start when you finish a Telnet session
which uses the letter G to access the games area,
and then log into another site that uses the same
letter to log off. Lose track of which site you're
visiting and such common irregularities can
become very annoying.

Most Telnet sites are very slow, but don't
worry, that's just the way it is. Fortunately, there
are a couple of ways to ensure more efficient
connections. Avoid using a Telnet site during
local business hours, because the machine is
often busy doing other tasks at this time. It's best
not to connect for long sessions because most
hosts have a limit on the number of guests who
can log on at any one time. Don't download
huge files just because they're there – make sure
you really need a file before downloading it. If a
site is always busy, or always very slow, it's worth
looking for another that offers similar services. If
you want to find out an e-mail address, Telnet to
the Knowbot at nri.reston.va.us using port 185.
The Knowbot is a huge database of e-mail information compiled from the NIC WHOIS database,
the PSA White Pages Pilot Project, MCI Mail and
the NYSERNET X.500 database.

Telnet for PC users

Because Telnet is slightly different to other
Internet tools, the URLs printed are slightly different too. As always, URLs in .net indicate we're
accessing our Telnet client from within a Web
browser like this: telnet://micros.hensa.ac.uk:
hensa (in fact, you only have to type in the first
part of the URL, like this: telnet://micros.hensa.
ac.uk).

The final part of the URL, after the colon, is the username you're prompted to enter when you connect to the Telnet site – in this case, the username is hensa. However, in most cases, Web browsers don't have Telnet connectivity built-in. They usually launch an external Telnet application and enter the URL directly into the client software.

If you're using a stand-alone Telnet program (there are several listed later in this chapter), ignore the telnet:// part of the URL. With most Windows clients, for example, you just enter the host name URL into a form. With this example you'd enter the following: micros.hensa.ac.uk

Press 'Enter' and wait for the connection to open. Once you're connected, enter hensa at the username prompt on-screen and you're in. That's all there is to it. You'll often need to enter a password, too. It's good manners to type in your e-mail address as the password.

Telnet for Mac users

Using Telnet on the Mac is much the same as using Telnet on the PC. You can start a session from within a Web browser, like Netscape Navigator, for instance, or run a stand-alone program like NSCA Telnet.

Because browsers don't have built-in Telnet ability, Netscape Navigator first launches your Telnet application, which then runs as if you'd launched it from the Finder. And because you're using a terminal emulator, Telnet sessions on all computer platforms are near enough the same. So everything we've said about URLs and logging on to Telnet systems above is exactly the same for all computer systems.

Try one of these...

International Telnet sites

• Archie:
telnet://archie.ans.net: archie

• CNI search:
telnet://gopher.cni.org: brsuser

• Electronic News Stand:
telnet://enews.com: news

• Gopher:
telnet://onsultant.micro.umn.edu: gopher

• HPCWire:
telnet://hpcwire.ans.net

• InterNIC Telnet:
telnet://ds.internic.net: guest

• NASA Extragalactic Database:
telnet://denver.ipac.caltech.edu: ned

• Netfind:
telnet://mudhoney.micro.umn.edu: netfind

• On-line Games Server:
telnet://castor.tat.physic.uni-tuebingen.de: games

• Oxford Dictionary of Familiar Quotations:
telnet://info.rutgers.edu: library: reference

• University of Michigan Library
English Dictionary:
telnet://cts.merit.edu: help

• White Pages/PSI:
telnet://wp.psi.net: fred

• Whois:
telnet://rs.internic.net

• World Wide Web:
telnet://info.cern.ch

• WorldWindow:
telnet://library.wustl.edu

UK Telnet sites

• BIRON:
telnet://biron.essex.ac.uk: biron

• HENSA – Higher Educational National Software
Archive:
telnet://micros.hensa.ac.uk: hensa

• JANET news:
telnet://news.janet.ac.uk: INFO

• Kings College Information Server:
telnet://info.kcl.ac.uk: INFO

• Loughborough University Information Server:
telnet://info.lut.ac.uk

• NISP:
telnet://mailbase.ac.uk: guest

• NISS – National Information Services and
Systems
telnet niss.ac.uk

• Oxford University OUCS Information Service:
telnet://info.ox.ac.uk

• Queen Mary & Westfield College Information
Server:
telnet://alpha.qmw.ac.uk: info

• SunSITE Northern Europe, Imperial College
Archie:
telnet://src.doc.ic.ac.uk: archie

• SunSITE Northern Europe, Imperial College
Archive:
telnet://src.doc.ic.ac.uk: sources

• University of Birmingham Campus Information
Service:
telnet://info.bham.ac.uk

• University of Bristol Information Server: telnet://info.bristol.ac.uk: info

• University of Edinburgh EdINFO: telnet://cas-
tle.ed.ac.uk: edinfo

• University of Southampton Campus
Information Service:
telnet://info.soton.ac.uk

• University of Wales, College of Cardiff
Information Server:
telnet://info.cf.ac.uk: info

• University of York Information Server:
telnet://info.york.ac.uk: INFO
Telnet software galore

If you're at university, some kind of Telnet software should already be available for you to use. If there isn't any, hassle your system administrator until he/she gives it to you. It works with our systems manager. If you're logging on from home, Telnet software should have been supplied by your Internet service provider in the software you received when you opened your account. If you haven't got any, for whatever reason, you can FTP it from these sites.

.net recommends

• DOS
ftp://micros.hensa.ac.uk/59/micros/ibmpc/dos/
f/f265/ and get cutcp1.zip, cutcp2.zip and
cutcp3.zip

• Windows
ftp://micros.hensa.ac.uk/59/micros/ibmpc/win/
e/e017/ewan104.zip

• Mac
ftp://micros.hensa.ac.uk/40/micros/mac/finder/
j/j164/j164ncsa.hqx

• Amiga
ftp://ftp.demon.co.uk/pub/amiga/anos29 – and
get the all files in the directory

• Atari ST
ftp://ftp.demon.co.uk/pub/atari/ka9q/
nos042_s.tos

Chapter 13

Future Publishing and the Internet

What's new   **Computing**   **Sport**   **Search**
What's hot   **Videogames**   **Music**   **Jobs**
What's cool   **Entertainment**   **Craft**   **Advertise**

FutureNet World News

Updates at around 1pm every weekday. Latest top stories:
- **World** - Euro ministers to discuss Bosnia
- **UK** - Labour demands tougher gun laws
- **Sport** - Cantona sets his sights on Europe

Latest hot features

Booze!
Everything you've ever wanted to know about alcohol on CD-ROMs and the Internet, from five steps to pouring Beamish Stout to a virtual breathalyser. Refill your knowledge with PC Review

Incoming!
The latest, most up to date Mac games release on the Internet. Find out exactly when IndyCar Racing 2, SimIsle, The 11 Hour and many others hit the streets and land on your Mac. Brought to you courtesy of MacFormat

The secrets of BBC radiophonics
The BBC department you've all heard: Quatermass, Dr Who, Hitch-Hiker's: Radiophonics (formerly the The Radiophonic Workshop). Now 40 years old, it opens its doors to Future Music

Pop into the Local to download your Guinness screen saver.

What's new | What's hot | What's cool | Search | Jobs | Advertise | About | Sponsors | Charities

FutureNet is © **Future Publishing**, maker of the world's finest print magazines...

Sport	**Videogames**	**Music**	**Computing**
Cycling Plus	Amiga Power	Classic CD	.net
Mountain Biking UK	EDGE	Future Music	The .net Directory
Mountain Biking Pro	GamesMaster	Total Guitar	Amiga Format
Total Football	PC Gamer		Amiga Shopper
Football Italia	PC Sports	**Craft**	CD-ROM Today
First XV	Sega Power	Cross Stitcher	Computer Arts
Boardstupid	SuperPlay	Cross Stitch Collection	MacFormat
	PlayStation	Good Woodworking	PC Answers
Entertainment	TOTAL!	Needlecraft	PC Format
arcane			PC Gamer
Comedy Review			PC Guide
SFX			PC Plus
			PC Review
			ST Format

Future Publishing is leading the UK publishing industry's charge on to the Internet with its FutureNet World Wide Web site which, last time we checked, was Europe's most accessed Web site. Point your World Wide Web browser at http://www.futurenet.co.uk/ and prepare to marvel at the naked beauty of the future of publishing.

FutureNet is changing by the day (as are most Web sites) so it's possible that some of this information will be out of date. But the following stuff represents the core of FutureNet and should always be there...

Registering for FutureNet

Although FutureNet is free to access, we do like to ask our kind visitors to register with us. The questions are very basic and you don't have to answer everything – and we only ask so we can find out more about our readers and tailor the site better to your needs.

FutureNet World News

A daily newswire with news stories from around the world updated at around 1pm every weekday. It's free, it's completely great and the showbiz news is second to none. Just like having a newspaper delivered to your desktop.

The Internet

Almost inevitably the most popular pages on FutureNet are the swimmingly bounteous creations from .net and The .net Directory. There are so many features, reviews and links here that you need never type in a URL again. Well, that's the idea anyway.

Computing

Overflowing with features, tips and advice from Britain's best computer magazines.

PC Format, PC Plus, PC Gamer, PC Guide, Mac Format, Amiga Format and many others are here in force, and there are numerous special subscription offers to save you cash.

Videogames

So many videogames magazines here it's almost a crime we don't bleed yer all for them.

But indeed, all the information from Sega Power, Edge, The Official PlayStation Magazine, GamesMaster, SuperPlay and PlayStation Power is here for you – free.

Sport

Future Publishing's ever-expanding skeletal empire now extends firmly into Dickie Davies land with hot titles such as Total Football, Rugby Union magazine First XV, and bike mags Cycling Plus, Mountain Biking UK and MTB Pro.

"Eat my goal!" as Alan Partridge would undoubtedly say.

Entertainment

There is only one science fiction magazine worth reading. It is called SFX and it is on the Web in style.

And there's the definitive guide to role-playing game resources on the Net thanks to the stunning new RPG magazine Arcane.

Music

Hey, rock 'n' roll, baby. And synthesiser pop. And classical music. Get features and loads more from riff-tastic Total Guitar, electro-tastic Future Music and dead-composer-tastic Classic CD.

Crafts

A stitch in time saves nine, and so does FutureNet. Top titles such as Needlecraft, Cross Stitcher and Cross Stitch Collection are here for the the wired needleperson in your life.

Security

FutureNet is running on a secure Netscape Web server, so if you're browsing with Netscape Navigator or a similar Web browser, your credit card details are scrambled before they're sent over the Net. This reduces the risk that credit card snoopers will pick up your card number to approximately nil. And just in case you missed it, All of this (and so very much more) is at

http://www.futurenet.co.uk/

Make FutureNet your home page and it won't let you down.

Chapter 14

The future of the Internet

This is the bit of the book where we get to indulge in some largely groundless speculation about the future of the Internet and its effects on us all.

There's no shortage of Net gurus attempting to beguile us with their own predictions, so to make it a fair fight, here's what we think…

Where do we start? What sort of timescale are we talking about? Looking two years into the future, the main impact – if it ever takes off – has to come from Java, or Java-based approaches. Why? Simply because Java allows creative types to do things that have never been done on the Net before. Initially, it's likely that Java will be confined to jazzing up Web pages as people begin to get to grips with the techniques. Although the Web is fine for linking lots of hypertext documents together, it's not always the most effective way of displaying information. You can easily get lost in the maze as you chase one interesting piece of information after another. Java will allow an extra dimension to Web pages and information to be displayed without getting too tangled in other Web pages.

But there's more than that to come. Java will allow new software applications to be developed although the real power of the system will only be apparent to very fast networks, like those found within corporations or scientific organisations. But what happens within companies today will filter onto the Net tomorrow, especially if the Net gets faster.

As far as Net Computers are concerned, people who see them portending the death of the personal computer are probably beating the wrong drum. PCs offer unrivalled flexibility to users and there's just too much invested in PC software for all that to be thrown away. However, what might happen is the Net Computer will be developed for alternative, smaller applications, where the PC is too overpowered to do the job. Handheld NCs linked to the Net via cellphones, dataterminals for newspapers, entertainment boxes – the future of the NC (and therefore much of the Internet) is in consumer electronics and not as a kind of stripped-down home computer. So both machines will exist side-by-side, in much the same way as videogames consoles coexist with personal computers.

Other Net-related applications in development include interactive live video and talk on-demand but at the moment it's unclear how this technology will benefit users. The Net is just too slow for this kind of thing to be generally available within the next 5-10 years. But as the telephone, cellphone, optical fibre and digital satellite TV networks become more integrated, major changes will be inevitable. Interactive videoconferencing technology for all will lead to big changes in the way we work, shop, select our medical services, vote and play. It may lead to weakened democracy as power filters away from centralised, regulated governments towards decentralised unregulated multinationals or networks of individuals – certainly, economic and political changes as a result of these technologies will be inevitable and there will be much to fight for. The process of globalisation, caused by cheap computer-based communications, has already had huge effects on employment, trade, economics and political integration. The Internet is another part of the process, and is where many of the new technologies and approaches to political issues, are being developed.

Whichever way it all turns out, one thing is for sure. The Internet, in one form or another, is here to stay. How it evolves is largely down to how people react to what it provides. If you want to be in on all that, reading this book has been a good start.

Index

Acorn users 44
alt newsgroups 60
alt.sex newsgroups 16
Amiga users 43
AmiTCP 43
Anarchie 77
Anonymous FTP .69
Applet 100, 103
Archie 74
ArcWeb 44, 90
ARPANET 13, 19
ASCII art 50
Atari ST users 43
Atlas 37
Attachment 50

BABT approval 23
Backbone 15
Baud rate 25
BBC Networking Club 61
BITNET 19
Bogomip 35, 37
Bookmark 80
Bounce 50
Browser 35, 80, 93, 99

Canter and Siegel 20
CCITT 25
CERN 80
Channel 108
CityScape 35
CityScape 38
CIX 27, 34, 38
Commercial service 34
Communications Decency Act 16
comp newsgroups 60
Compression 71
CompuServe 18, 26, 34, 38

CSNET 19

Demon 33, 36, 38, 43
Discussion groups 58
Domain 48
Domain name 41, 49

E-mail 19,33, 46, 53, 86
E-mail address 48
Easynet 38
EFNet 107
EFNet servers 109
Enclosure 50
ETLA 64
Eudora 35, 54
EUnet 19
Express 28.8E fax/modem 29

FAQ (Frequently Asked Question) 62
Fax modem 27
FidoNet 19
Flame 64
Free Agent 65
Freeware 88
FTP 35, 52, 68, 86
FTP mail 52
Future Publishing 18, 127
FutureNet 127

Gopher 20, 68, 72, 82, 86
Grapevine 113

Home page 87
Homer 113
HotJava 103
HQX format 71
HTML .15, 81, 87, 92
http:// 87

https:// 88
Hyperlink 82
Hypertext 80, 93

IBM 38
Internet 9, 19
    future of the Internet 132
    history of the Internet 12, 19
Internet Society, the 15, 49
Internet Worm 19
Internews 65
IP (Internet Protocol) 12
IP address 49
IRC (Internet Relay Chat) 106
IRC client 113
IRC commands 110
Ircle 113
JANET 19
Java 98, 103, 132
JavaStation 101

Knowbot 118

Libel 64
Link 88
Linnet 34 fx 29
Listserv 51
Lynx 87

Mac Internet Starter Kit 42
Mac Internet Tour Guide 42
Macintosh users 37, 42
MacTCP 42
MacWeb 89
Mail-It 35
Mailing list 51
Majordomo 51
MBONE 20

Microsoft Network 18
MIME 50
Mirror 70, 83, 88
Mobifax 144 28
Modem 22, 35
    internal modem .24
    PCMCIA modem card 24
Mosaic 35, 88, 94

NC (Network Computer) 99, 103, 133
Net Nanny 61
Netiquette 50, 62
netkonect 38
Netscape 20, 35, 81, 88
news newsgroups 60
News server 58
Newsbse 0.50 55
Newsgroup 33, 58, 85
Newsreader 59
Newswatcher 65
NSF (National Science Foundation) 14
NSFNET 14, 19

Oasis 55
Off-line 49

Pavilion 33, 38
PC users 42
PCElm 55
Pipex 33, 35, 38
PoP 32
POP3 48
Pornography 61
Power PK-2880M 29

QuarkXPress 95

rec newsgroups 60

RedNet 38

sci newsgroups 60
Service provider 32
Shareware 88
Shouting 63
Signature 50, 63
Slander 64
Smileys 64
SMTP 48
Snews 65
soc newsgroups 60
Spamming 63
Sportster 14,400 .28
Sportster 28,800 .29

TCP/IP 14
Telnet 116
    International Telnet sites 120
    UK Telnet sites .121
TLA 64
Tornado 14,400 fax/modem 28
Tornado FM288E .29
Turbogopher 77

uk newsgroups 60
UK On-Line .18, 34
Undernet 107
Undernet servers 110
UNIX 13, 70
URL 84, 88
Usenet 19, 33, 58
User to modem ratio 36
UUencoding .52, 61

V.Fast Class 26
V22 25
V22bis 25

V32 25
V32 Terbo 26
V32bis 25
V34 25
V42 25
V42bis 25
Veronica 74

WAIS 20, 76, 82
Web IRC 114
Webster 44, 90
WinWeb for Windows 89
World Wide Web 18, 20, 33, 53, 80
WS FTP 77
WS Gopher 77
WSIRC for Windows 113

Zetnet 33

.net is the best and best-selling Internet magazine in Britain because it exists purely to provide you with information about the on-line world that is more reliable, relevant, practical and incisive than any other magazine you can buy.

NO RISK TRIAL
Subscribe today and get 3 trial issues- If you decide to cancel your subscription to *.net* within the first three months, we will give you a full refund, no questions asked. Plus you'll save money – we'll give you 12 issues for the price of 10.

12 issues **for the price of 10**

Please send me 12 issues of *.net*   ❑ £30 (UK only)

overseas rates available on application.

I can receive a full refund up to 5 days after receipt of my third issue.

Title_____Initials_____ Surname_____

Address_____

_____ Post code _____

Daytime Tel: _____

Please select your preferred method of payment:

❑ **CHEQUE** A Cheque is enclosed for £_____ payable to **Future Publishing Ltd**

❑ **CREDIT CARD** Please charge my   ❑ VISA   ❑ MASTERCARD

Card number_____expiry date _____

Date _____ Signature _____

SUBSCRIPTION HOTLINE: **0 1 2 2 5   8 2 2 5 1 1**
(weekdays 8.45-6pm) FAX: **0 1 4 5 8   2 7 4 3 7 8**

Please reply to: .net Subscriptions **FREEPOST** (BS4900), Somerton, Somerset, TA11 6BR.

E-mail subs@futurenet.co.uk

Please tick here if you would prefer not to receive details of new products and offers.

INTB605